a handbook for media librarians

edited by **Katharine Schopflin**

facet publishing

Published by Facet Publishing, 7 Ridgmount Street, London WC1E 7AE
www.facetpublishing.co.uk

Facet Publishing is wholly owned by CILIP: the Chartered Institute of Library
and Information Professionals.

British Library Cataloguing in Publication Data
A catalogue record for this book is available from the British Library.

ISBN 978-1-85604-630-5

First published 2008

Typeset from author's disk in 11/14pt University Old Style and Zurich Expanded
by Facet Publishing.
Printed and made in Great Britain by MPG Books Ltd, Bodmin, Cornwall.

Contents

Contributors

Graeme Boyd is Librarian at Greenpeace International. His background is in magazines, mainly fashion photography (Condé Nast) and environmental photography (Greenpeace), but he has had experience in all types of library settings from library assistant (the Glasgow School of Art) to information researcher (BBC).

Carol Bradley Bursack is a newspaper librarian and elder care columnist living in Fargo, North Dakota, USA. She is the author of *Minding Our Elders: caregivers share their personal stories* (published by McCleery and Sons Publishing, 2005). She speaks on caregiving issues, and has a blog and website, under the brand 'Minding Our Elders'.

Katy Heslop joined the research department of the *Guardian* and *Observer* in 2000 as a trainee librarian. After graduating from the MSc Information Science course at City University in 2002, she returned to the *Guardian* as a researcher. She is deputy editor of ResearchNet, the library intranet, and manages the library team that helped to develop the Guardian and Observer Digital Archive.

Colin Hunt entered librarianship as a branch library junior in Liverpool in 1963. After qualifying as a Chartered librarian he held a number of specialist posts in public and industrial libraries. He joined the *Liverpool Daily Post and Echo* in 1973 where, as Head of Library Services, he has at various times had responsibility for exhibitions, photosales and special publications. He has written several books on Merseyside and co-authored or researched many more; he has lectured on news librarianship at both Liverpool John Moores and Manchester Metropolitan universities. For relaxation he plays blues guitar at any venue that will book him. He has a grown-up family and lives on Wirral.

Linda MacDonald graduated with an MSc in Information and Library Studies in 2000. In 2002, after 18 months as information officer at the Institute of Practitioners in Advertising, she joined the *Guardian* and *Observer*'s research department as a news researcher. She is also editor of the department's intranet and manages content on Guardian Unlimited's Freedom of Information site. She is a Chartered librarian and has been events organizer for the Association of UK Media Librarians since 2006.

Joanne Playfoot did a BA Library and Information Studies course at the University of Brighton, graduating in 1998. She joined London listings magazine *Time Out* magazine in the same year as a library trainee. In 1999 she moved to IPC Magazines progressing from the post of information assistant, to information officer and becoming library and research manager in 2005.

Katharine Schopflin has worked for the BBC and ITN Source. A media librarian with ten years' experience, she was the Chair of the Association of UK Media Librarians (AUKML) between 2005 and 2007. She regularly contributes articles to the professional informaton press and is currently working on a part-time research degree at University College London's School of Library, Archive and Information Studies.

Hazel Simpson has been with the BBC's Information & Archives department since 1988. Her work has covered television, news, sound and written archives as a cataloguer and a researcher. She has been studying with the Open University since 2001 and hopes that by the end of 2008 she will possess a BA (Honours) in Humanities with History of Science and Technology.

Ian Watson was Information Services Manager and Head of Rights and Information with Glasgow's *Herald* and *Evening Times* newspapers under three ownership regimes between 1994 and 2006. He is currently Knowledge and Information Manager with the Scottish Institute for Excellence in Social Work Education. He was chair of the Association of UK Media Librarians (AUKML) between 2001 and 2003.

Chapter 1

Media libraries in the 21st century

KATHARINE SCHOPFLIN

The purpose of this book is to explore the main issues facing information workers employed by media organizations, that is, broadcasters and publishers of newspapers, magazines and websites. Each chapter examines an issue that librarians, archivists, cataloguers, researchers and other information professionals are likely to face in their working life, with chapters written by practitioners who have faced these problems themselves. The aim is to spread knowledge acquired through practical experience to help solve and prevent problems as they arise. 'Media librarian' in this book does not refer to those looking after multimedia collections in public or academic libraries, although some of the issues discussed may be useful to them. In addition, although controversial among practitioners, the author uses the term 'media librarians' to refer to all who carry out information work for media organizations (although their actual job title may be 'Researcher', 'Media Manager' or 'Information Manager', for example) for historical reasons, for convenience and because she has never considered libraries to be exclusively collections of books.

Media librarians have a low profile in the information profession and among their employers. Academic, legal and public librarians are often intrigued to discover that some of their peers work for the same people who provide their television programmes and daily newspaper. Journalists write articles perpetuating the idea that libraries are dusty book collections run by stern ladies with date stamps, unaware that the people who provided their newspaper database or background research are part of this profession.

Yet media companies, producing vast quantities of content in an increasing variety of formats, need people both to help them fill up column inches, pages or hours, and to organize this content afterwards so that it can be found again. The profession offering the best skills to meet that need is librarianship and information services. Librarians are the specialists in connecting people who work in media companies with the items they need to do their jobs and putting it where they can find it again. Although unlikely to be called librarians or, in the 21st century, to be working in a room called 'the library', information professionals continue to carry out this task for media organizations throughout the world.

A short history

The media librarian's role has changed significantly since the days of newspaper 'morgues' – cuttings collections filed by subject and personality by clerical staff, where reluctant trainee journalists often had to spend a few months before being allowed to write their first stories. In the 1980s they were among the earliest adopters of online databases, in those days dial-up connections to news databases such as FT Profile. It was during these years that the sector sought to professionalize itself and, for the first time, the news library employee became as likely to have graduated from library school as to have arrived in the company as a 16-year-old clerk.

In the late 1990s online databases began to be accessible through the world wide web. Being able to search via the company intranet was a time-saving boon to librarians, but the databases were now also available to journalists and programme-makers directly. Because end-users now had direct access to information sources previously only searched by librarians, the latter lost their role as gatekeepers and intermediaries between their users and their research resources. Although new roles associated with online research appeared, such as training, subscription management and web content management, many librarians found it a struggle to keep those roles within the library. It was harder still to justify the existence of mediated researchers and prove that they had special skills not held by their customers who, after all, tended to be journalists who prided themselves on their research skills.

The results of these changes varied from organization to organization. In some cases, managing and controlling subscriptions, catalogues and research intranets raised the library's profile, made them seem relevant to younger journalists and even resulted in an increase in enquiry numbers (various examples are given in Schopflin and Nelsson, 2007). In others, the fact that journalists and programme-makers could access research tools without using the library convinced many managers and budget-owners that specialist staff were no longer needed. The same issues began to affect those managing audiovisual collections. Once programmes began to be created on servers in the newsroom and accessible online, it appeared to senior management that specialist film researchers were unnecessary and even programme metadata could be added by the programme-makers themselves. In some organizations the role of the archive was reduced to managing the retrieval of pre-digital legacy formats.

Despite the best efforts of many library managers to convince their paymasters of the value of skilled professional staff, a depressing number of units closed in the late 1990s and early 2000s. Those that survived did so through a mixture of communication, diversification and, especially, promotion. Classic methods, such as posters and leaflets, becoming part of the company induction and holding 'brown bag lunches' proved useful to many. For others training journalists and programme-makers in the use of online databases provided a showcase for library skills. As one veteran media librarian noted, 'journalists are prepared to wade through pages of drivel rather than ask for help' (Dunn, 2005). Demonstrating search methods and how to evaluate and choose research sources was one means of showing users that they were not as accomplished in online searching as they thought. Moreover, such sessions became a means of publicizing collections which were not available to the end-user, such as newspaper cuttings archives or periodical collections. One media librarian noted an increase in enquiry numbers after databases were rolled out to end-users as they used induction sessions to promote the range of their services and holdings, of which many journalists were unaware (Schopflin and Nelsson, 2007).

Like most workplace libraries, media libraries were also subject to changes affecting their parent organizations. The media industry was particularly hard-pressed in the 1990s and early 2000s by globalization, deregulation, the challenges of maintaining advertising income in a time of proliferation of new media, conglomeration and cuts to the public sector. In the early 2000s, commercial media organizations perceived themselves to be in crisis following 'the worst advertising recession in 30 years' (Cassey, 2002). Public sector organizations (for example the British Broadcasting Corporation, BBC) faced different pressures, finding it difficult to justify public funding as their audience fragmented, both to increasing numbers of other television channels, and to new activities presented to consumers, for example by video recorder and internet.

Global newspaper circulation was in long-term decline (Greenslade, 2003) and publications feared competition from the world wide web. One journalist remarked that 'as the amount of information available online explodes, papers will inevitably face a losing fight to hold on to readers' (Greenslade, 2003). Conglomeration, particularly among regional newspapers and commercial broadcasting, gave large media companies the opportunity to merge and downsize departments and make many staff redundant. In the face of this insecurity, the library and information unit was the most vulnerable part of the organization, particularly where the perception was held that new technology meant library skills were no longer needed.

The late 2000s are without doubt an interesting time for media librarians. But despite the challenges the profession faces in convincing broadcasters and publishers that their skills are vital to the authority, depth and quality of their output, repeated predictions of the death of the media library have been exaggerated. Media channels proliferate interactive and portable formats, needing well researched content and to be made accessible in the future. Although financial managers will always attempt to cut the cake of human capital in new ways in the hope that they can save on headcount, research and archiving remain necessary. Many are realizing that perhaps the most efficient and cheapest way to accomplish it is to pay information professionals to carry it out. Those library and information units that survive and flourish are those which have spread this message to the people who matter within their organizations.

Characteristics of media libraries

Information work in the media industry is centred around two main areas. First, librarians help provide content for what is published or broadcast by their parent company. This might be fact-checking, in-depth information research, providing research sources online, finding archive pictures or clearing stills for use. Second, they help to process, maintain and organize what is produced by the organization, so that this material can be found again and possibly commercially exploited. All media organizations require these tasks to be carried out. What varies is how much is given to information-related departments, how much to journalists and programme-makers, how much to administrative staff and how much is outsourced.

The working environment

Media libraries and information units bear little resemblance to the traditional idea of the library. Like many corporate libraries, they have been under pressure to give up precious office space and it is rare to see a media library today with many paper-based holdings. Those concentrating mainly on research are likely to have some reference books either not available online or more economically purchased in hard copy. Magazine and broadcasting libraries often stock periodicals not available through commercial databases or which may be used for reference or rostruming (that is filming for television broadcast). However, the vast majority of media libraries look like every other office in the building. Even those professionals managing the tape archives belonging to broadcasting organizations are under pressure to store non-essential items off site and are normally based in basements and other unglamorous areas of their company's offices.

As with other corporate research units, media libraries primarily carrying out enquiry work are noisy, busy places. Even where the bulk of enquiry work is done by e-mail, or the main tasks are cataloguing, it is rare to encounter a 'library hush' in a media organization. Most media librarians are accustomed to working to very tight deadlines, often matters of minutes where some information or archive may be needed for immediate transmission. This can lead their users to have unrealistic expectations when they use specialist libraries primarily catering to the research and academic communities. Because of publication or transmission requirements, media libraries are often staffed at odd times of day. Today only a few news research units are open 24 hours a day, seven days a week, but even those that offer users a reduced number of hours of research backup will be open at weekends and evenings if this is useful for their deadlines. Information units archiving, cataloguing or indexing content for newsrooms may also run seven-day operations so that published or broadcast material can be reused or sold on as soon as possible.

Most media library jobs are within the commercial sector. Whereas the legal business information communities have academic and professional libraries in addition to corporate information units within individual organizations, there is no public sector equivalent for media libraries (as currently defined). This means there is no centre of excellence operating as a knowledge- or skills-base outside the commercial sector. Admittedly, the UK's one public-sector employer of media librarians, the BBC, employs the largest number of people carrying out information work in the sector (as might be expected for a multi-channel, multimedia 24-hour broadcaster). However, its stated aims are to broadcast and produce radio and television programmes and web and interactive content to public sector standards. This does not mean that professional work is required to be of the highest standard across the board. Indeed, information services are seen as an overhead, diverting money from the core activity of broadcasting.

Media library users

Corporate libraries take their character from their parent organization and users of information services differ considerably depending on whether they practise law, industrial research, property management, high finance, charitable activities or any number of commercial or public services. The largest group of users of media library services are journalists and broadcasters and, although clearly there are huge variations from organization to organization, those who are attracted to such jobs can be characterized as being creative rather than analytical or introspective. The task of assembling research materials tends to be carried out by those at a more junior level, by staff who are often young, inexperienced and still learning to cope with pressure from superiors. Media librarians need to accustom themselves to brusque treatment and an inexperienced approach to knowledge-seeking from their customers. However, the creative community also includes people with huge amounts of subject or technical knowledge and it is often they who are the most appreciative of what information professionals are capable of (even if they do not quite understand it). The author has written more on the users of media libraries in the Association of UK Media Librarians (AUKML) newsletter *Deadline* (Schopflin, 2005).

Types of media library
Newspaper and magazine libraries

Most of the larger newspaper groups had a library at one point although many have been closed or downsized. The remaining libraries vary from large units supporting prestigious daily or weekly titles (in the UK, examples are held at the *Guardian* or News International) to individuals working solo for small local papers, many part of large media groups (regional newspapers in the USA and the UK are controlled by a very small number of companies). Their work is generally divided into four areas: information research, archiving newspaper content for in-house use or sale to news aggregation services, managing stills collections (whether sourcing and licensing commercial stills or managing an archive possibly including items whose copyright is owned by the newspaper) and managing subscriptions for the newsroom to use. Other responsibilities include compiling in-house specialist information sources, current awareness monitoring and training end-users on the use of subscription or in-house databases. Few units carry out the traditional task of classifying hard copy newspaper articles, as the vast majority of newspaper articles are retrievable from newspaper text databases. However, most have retained their cuttings archives for historical research and commercial exploitation.

Magazine libraries' activities cover much the same areas as newspapers: information research, archiving, subscription management and looking after stills collections. However, magazine content requires either more in-depth analysis (for current affairs magazines) or more lifestyle content (for consumer magazines). They may also require visually stimulating material such as graphics and stills, whose research or syndication may be carried out by library staff. Customer relationships in magazine-publishing organizations are likely to differ from those in newspapers as, rather than supporting teams producing primarily in-house content for a small number of daily or weekly titles, magazine libraries often provide services for hundreds of titles a month, each with different deadlines, covering a huge range of topics and in many cases operating more as commissioners than writers. Perhaps because of this, some magazine groups have never had information or research units. These organizations rely on a mixture of end-user databases and outsourcing to carry out their research and archiving tasks.

Television libraries

Television organizations tend to have separate areas for information research and archives if, indeed, both areas are carried out by information professionals. Information research units are run much like units of newspaper publishers although they may be open for longer hours and offer a more diverse range of services. The main difference will be the requirement to source newspaper and magazine articles for rostruming (filming), a small but important part of any television information researcher's job. Also significant is that in many cases the content produced by the organization may not be news, but lifestyle programmes, documentaries, music or even drama, all of which require slightly different sets of research priorities.

Any organization that produces broadcast content needs to keep and access it in some way so that content can be reused and resold. Every production or broadcasting company has someone looking after their footage (also known as 'media assets') for broadcast and reuse, even if this is an unpaid runner or intern. Formats covered might include film, videotape, server files or website plugins. The costs of storage and access mean that few television organizations keep all of the programmes they have made but most keep some. In the UK, broadcasters are required to keep all output for three months for legal reasons, something which is often carried out by library technical staff. Television and radio archives require technical work, storage, cataloguing and copyright licensing. They also need to find material for reuse or commercial exploitation. However, these tasks are increasingly carried out, to greater or lesser professional standards, by journalists or specialist researchers in the newsroom, the latter of whom may or may not identify themselves as information professionals.

Most large media organizations now own a variety of content platforms including newspapers, magazines, web services and broadcasting companies. However, they are often run as entirely separate companies (as with News International newspapers and British Sky Broadcasting, both owned by NewsCorp, or the various parts of the AOL-TimeWarner conglomerate). In other cases information services originally provided for newspapers or magazines changed when, for example, web services or book publishing were added to the company's portfolio. Another trend is that new departments appear, but their staff are unaware of the library, or not able to use it under existing service level agreements. It is rare, however, for an organization to redesign an information service completely in order to meet the needs of an expanded multimedia organization.

Media librarianship as a profession
Media librarianship and the information profession

In some ways, media librarians are among the least connected of all sectors to the wider information profession. Many who carry out research or information-related activities do not identify themselves as information professionals at all. There are a variety of reasons for this. First, the traditional career trajectory of those in media libraries was to work as clerks cutting and filing articles (or reshelving tapes), then move on to classifying newspapers and answering enquiries, without spending an obligatory year studying librarianship. Although this has changed in some organizations, it is not uncommon for there to be no qualification requirement in media library job advertisements. This not only demotivates media librarians from becoming involved with the wider profession, but also helps to establish a culture whereby both staff and managers feel that wider professional skills and knowledge are irrelevant. Clearly this varies from unit to unit. Many media library managers are members of professional associations and are committed to allowing their staff to grow as skilled professionals rather than simply as staff. However, media library staff often struggle to be released for daytime training events or given the chance to attend external courses.

Furthermore, because of the perceived glamour of the sector and the shortage of jobs in the media industry, some see information work as an entrance route to the core creative activities of the organization rather than greater professional advancement. These people perceive librarians as subordinate to production staff or journalists (even if the latter are no better paid or graded). Ironically, the route from the library to the newsroom or production office has become more open in recent years. Now that journalists and programme-makers are expected to carry out some or all of their research themselves, and in many cases to provide their output with metadata or rudimentary cataloguing, organizational and research skills are more valued in end-user departments. However, the jobs themselves are designated as journalistic or production positions rather than information roles.

Career prospects

At the time of writing there is no doubt that the pool of jobs in media information units is shrinking. As previously stated, media organizations have used financial pressures and new technologies as opportunities to reduce headcount. However, whereas in the early 2000s entire units were being closed for good, it is now more likely that individual posts may be lost and these can sometimes subsequently be claimed back. Moreover there are now roles in other parts of the organization, notably among researchers, information architects and professionals working with metadata, who carry out roles requiring information skills. Whether the incumbents practise the roles to professional standards, or identify themselves (secretly or openly) as information professionals, is another matter.

A new entrant to the profession is less likely than otherwise to be joining something called a library or resembling the traditional idea of one. There remain a few large 24-hour or seven-day news research or cataloguing units, but the large teams of researchers who constituted the bulk of media librarians in the 1980s and 1990s are the exception rather than the rule in the 21st century. More often, teams of two or three professionals work in offices which may even be collocated with those of their customers. There are very few clerical positions available in any library and those that exist tend to be limited to stock retrieval in audiovisual collections and newspaper data archiving. In both cases there are increasingly fewer positions as demand is expected to shrink either through outsourcing or automation, or because of end-user online access to media assets. This means that most people start their media library careers carrying out professional jobs.

Because teams are smaller, there are fewer opportunities for promotion by the traditional route of managing staff. However, the purchasing and implementation of new technology gives rise to a significant number of project-related jobs (although in many cases the information unit's contributions will be given by existing staff in addition to their ordinary jobs). As previously mentioned, many information professionals now also move sideways to jobs on the production or journalistic side of the organization, something which was previously very rare. In production areas, there may be more upward mobility and the jobs are often better paid and of higher status (without requiring a greater degree of skill). There is, however, anecdotal evidence that information staff may have more job security and better working hours than those working in newsrooms and production offices.

Salaries

Compared with many workplace libraries, the salary differential between media librarians and their users is less marked than, for example, in the legal and business sector. However, media librarians are in general paid less than information professionals working in legal or financial services companies or even for government departments. Although organizations' pay policies vary, an entry level salary is likely to be similar to that of an academic library. Unlike academic libraries, the absence of specialist posts means earning potential is not as high. However, a media librarian is likely to earn more than their equivalents in art, museum and learned society libraries and, in many cases, than those in public libraries.

Training

Because of the lack of professional recognition within media organizations, chartership and, in some organizations, even library qualifications are unnecessary. However, a library and information studies course is likely to give potential employees the best preparation for professional work in media libraries. In the UK there is only one course, at City University, which has a specific option in media librarianship. However, most recognized information courses will offer compulsory or optional modules that are useful.

A good grounding in research techniques, online and field searching and different information sources is essential for any information or archive research position. It is also important to demonstrate an ability to judge the authoritativeness of a particular source. Those working with audiovisual material often need cataloguing skills (although the principles are more important than any particular cataloguing system) and it will be particularly useful if the course covers the cataloguing of non-traditional materials. A film archiving course may be as appropriate as a librarianship degree for these positions. Trends change quickly in the information world. At the time of writing, any course that offers introductions to web design, information architecture or media asset management would make a candidate highly employable by media libraries. But it is worth remembering that any proprietary software used at university is likely to be very different by the time a student is employed to carry out this kind of work. Media librarians also need to have a good knowledge of current affairs and, increasingly, the world of showbiz and celebrities. In fact, an interest in these areas is a prerequisite for working in the sector and candidates are likely to be tested on this in job interviews.

Once in the workplace, media librarians often have few opportunities for training, as budgets are frequently tight and there are few opportunities to be released to attend courses. However, media librarians need to be aware of changes both in the profession and in the needs of the organization and wider industry, to constantly refresh and build on their skills to adapt to the future needs of their employers (and those of future employers). Current skills and knowledge in demand include training end-users, writing for the web, following developments in media asset management, knowledge of copyright, and managing and negotiating contracts. Where in-house training is unavailable, professional associations and publications can fill the gap.

Professional associations

The largest organization devoted to media librarianship is the News Division (www.ibiblio.org/slanews) of the US-based (but internationally focussed) SLA (Special Libraries Association), which represents librarians in the workplace sector (not working for public or academic libraries). SLA is a large and influential organization, which holds a highly regarded conference in the USA and carries out many other networking and information-sharing activities. Its News Division is considered to be among the more lively sections and without a doubt represents the world's largest body of media librarians (albeit with a slant towards hard news rather than the looser definition of media librarians). For those unable to pay SLA subscriptions, it is free to join the busy and informative News Division e-mail discussion list, NewsLib (http://parklibrary.jomc.unc.edu/newsliblyris. html), and they also have a blog (http://newslib.blogspot.com). In the UK, AUKML (the Association of UK Media Librarians, of which the current author is ex-chair; www.aukml.org.uk) is a small, independent voluntary professional association with no corporate membership, but a range of professional activities available free to members. Like the News Division, AUKML publishes a newsletter and runs an e-mail discussion group.

As an alternative to specialized media librarian groups, or in countries where one does not exist, networking opportunities should be available through organizations representing the special or workplace sector of the information profession (the function performed by SLA in the USA). In the UK the main organization is the Commercial, Legal and Scientific Group (CLSG; www.cilip.org.uk/specialinterestgroups/bysubject/iclg), one of the largest groups of the UK lead industry body, the Chartered Institute of Library and Information Professionals (CILIP). CLSG organizes a range of events aimed broadly at those carrying out information work in a business or commercial environment and has the financial and institutional backing of a fully staffed chartered association. It is possible to join CLSG without joining CILIP.

Other relevant associations are cross-sectoral organizations representing stills and audiovisual collections and their researchers. In the UK, these are FOCAL (www.focalint.org), which represents footage libraries and film researchers (especially those working freelance) and has an international presence, the Picture Research Association (PRA; www.picture-research. org.uk) and BAPLA, the British Association for Libraries and Pictures Agencies (www.bapla.org.uk). In the USA, the lead body is the Association of Moving Image Archivists (www.amianet.org). There are also two important international organizations, the International Federation of Film Archives (FIAF; www.fiafnet.org) and the International Federation of Television Archives (FIAT; www.fiatifta.org). These organizations hold events attended by representatives of the world's major audiovisual collections in order to set policy and discuss new developments.

Less formal networking and information-sharing activities also take place in the media library world. There are a range of blogs aimed at keeping the profession up to date, with search resources (such as Gary Price's ResourceShelf, www.resourceshelf.com) or with general issues of interests like the NewsLib blog and the Gaol House Blog (http:// gaolhouseblog.blogspot.com). The largest single area of social networking in the media library world is the NewsLib discussion list. On this busy list research questions, matters of policy, new technology, and sources and items of general interest to those working in the sector are discussed; although it is a US-based organization, membership is international.

Literature

There has been very little formal publication on the subject of media librarianship since Paula Hane's *Super Searchers in the News* (Hane, 2000) rounded up the essential online resources used by news researchers. The last general guide in English was respected US library academic Barbara Semonche's *News Media Libraries* in 1993 (Semonche, 1993). In 2006 the author collaborated on the media libraries chapter of the latest edition of the *Survey of British Library and Information Work* (Bowman, 2007). There has been more writing in professional journals, including not only association newsletters such as *Deadline* and *News Library News* but also articles in broader industry publications such as *Library + Information Update*, *Library Journal*, *American Libraries* and *Library and Information Science Research*. However, the greatest wealth of writing, and the most up-to-date survey of the issues at the heart of the profession, are to be found in the archives of the News Lib e-mail discussion list.

Policy for media libraries

Workplace libraries are subject to the whims and stresses of their parent organization and industry sector. It can therefore be difficult for them to formulate a policy which can be carried across different units within the sector. Attempts have been made: former AUKML chair Helen Martin has written about the early days of the Association, circa 1986, when the group acted as a think tank composed of information managers who could return directly to their library and implement policy decided at a committee meeting (Martin, 2004). It is far harder to achieve this against a background of organizational change and strictures. Moreover, the notion of what a 'media library' is has changed beyond recognition since those days. There is evidence that the SLA News Division has more success at laying down policy at the annual SLA conference (www.ibiblio.org/slanews/conferences).

However, media librarians at all levels implement policy every working day. Questions like 'What resource should I buy?', 'Shall I let this user borrow this item?', 'Is it ethical for me to answer that question?' or 'How can I describe this footage?' set policy and precedent every day. That they do not do it in a vacuum is a tribute to the professional networks, formal and informal, which connect the profession. Similar to most in the profession, media librarians like to share experiences and offer advice to their peers. It is the aim of this book to condense and synthesize some of this invaluable knowledge so that today's media librarians are equipped to face the issues that affect them every day at work.

References

Bowman, J. (2007) *Survey of British Library and Information Work*, Ashgate.

Cassey, J. (2002) Where's the Cash?, *Guardian*, (19 August).

Dunn, J. (2005) If Media Libraries Didn't Exist We Would Have to Invent Them. In *AUKML 2005 Conference: Essential Skills for Information* (12 March).

Greenslade, R. (2003) The Shape of Things to Come?, *Guardian*, (10 November).

Hane, P. (2000) *Super Searchers in the News*, CyberAge Books.

Martin, H. (2004) Letter to the Editor, *Deadline*, (March).

Nelsson, R. and Schopflin K. (2007) Media Libraries. In *Survey of British Library and Information Work*, Ashgate.

Schopflin, K. (2005) Working for Creatives, *Deadline*, (December).

Semonche, B. (1993) *News Media Librarianship: a management handbook* (Greenwood Press).

Chapter 2

The virtual media library (I): managing intranets

LINDA MacDONALD and KATY HESLOP

As journalists have turned from ordering press cuttings files from their organization's library to accessing their information online, new roles have emerged for media librarians to apply their traditional research and organizational skills to the online world. This chapter intends to demonstrate the value of research intranets to media libraries and organizations, and provide library practitioners with an idea of best practice in terms of creating and maintaining such a resource. The authors are part of the Guardian's Research and Information Department; they were directly involved with the relaunch of their research intranet and are now responsible for its ongoing management.

The chapter examines what a research intranet is, the history of intranets in media libraries and how these have evolved to become resources used by leading media organizations. A successful research intranet depends on a number of factors, which range from content and design to user-testing and marketing. By demonstrating and assessing how specific media libraries are using and developing their intranets this chapter gives library practitioners guidelines about managing intranets and meeting user needs. The increasing sophistication of information technology and the rise of Web 2.0 applications offer greater opportunities to enhance intranet development. It is the authors' belief that, as media librarians, they are ideally equipped to take advantage of these.

Introduction and history

According to the *Oxford English Dictionary* (*OED*) an intranet is a 'local or restricted computer network; spec. a private or corporate network that uses Internet protocols'. As a website intended solely for internal use, its content is produced by the organization, for the organization, in order to communicate effectively the issues which affect its members. Intranets promote knowledge-sharing and provide a single and secure point of access, allowing a company to manage its information and reduce the cost of information sourcing, printing and distribution. Intranet content can include staff directories, policies and procedures, bulletin boards, staff discounts and activities. Available and accessible to all members of an organization, an intranet is an ideal platform on which a smaller department such as a library can make its presence felt.

In the mid-1990s UK commercial and public sector organizations embraced intranet technology. A survey published by KPMG in 1997 (quoted in White, 1998) revealed that among 100 large companies 48% of respondents had installed an intranet, and 37% would do so over the next three years. During the same period, library intranets had started to become a common feature in media organizations, especially in the USA. By 1996 British news organizations such as News International, the *Herald* and the *Guardian* were developing intranets. These early sites usually consisted of very simple pages filled with text and hyperlinks on plain backgrounds. Constructed using basic HTML (hypertext markup language) they were restricted in terms of aesthetics, navigation and functionality. Lists of useful websites were a prominent feature as, in the pre-Google days, it was recognized that users struggled to find accurate and authoritative sources.

The *Guardian*'s research intranet

The *Guardian*'s research intranet, managed by the library (or Research Department as it was called), was launched in 1999 and called ResearchNet (Figure 2.1 on next page).

By 2003 it was apparent that, although it offered some valuable features, the intranet's current format no longer met the demands of editorial staff, now more adept at internet searching and eagerly embracing Google. The *Guardian* relaunched its company intranet as Spike, giving staff access to information including a staff directory, electronic noticeboards, a list of staff activities and discounts, as well as areas for specific departments such as

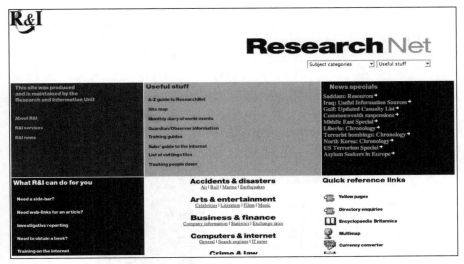

Figure 2.1   ResearchNet in 1999

Human Resources and Information Technology. The Research Department took the opportunity to redevelop and relaunch ResearchNet.

As part of the development, they undertook an audit of resources, deciding which to discard and retain as well as investigating new features to add. The Spike team, part of the *Guardian*'s press office, offered invaluable training and technical expertise to help create a more sophisticated design, including pictures, and reflecting the *Guardian*'s corporate style. Incorporated within Spike, ResearchNet now has a far greater audience reach; it is included on Spike's search engine and has a high-profile location on the home page. Co-operation, guidance and endorsement from other stakeholders made the redesign possible, but the day-to-day management of ResearchNet is left entirely to the Research Department, which has many other priorities to deal with. As this chapter will demonstrate, maintaining a current, accurate and engaging intranet is a challenge and often an ongoing process of re-evaluating resources against evolving user needs. Figure 2.2 on the next page shows the home page of ResearchNet in 2007.

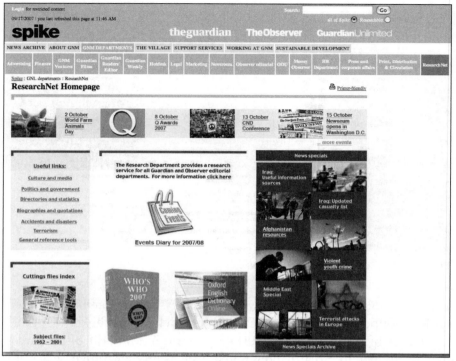

Figure 2.2   ResearchNet home page in 2007

Creating your intranet
Setting out your objectives

Before you set about creating an intranet, it is important to draw up a plan
outlining your objectives. Think about why you want to set it up. Have you
identified a real need to provide information to your users? Have users, or
management, requested one? Or do you feel that it's something you should
be doing, but aren't really sure why? Working through the following
questions will help you focus on the type of intranet you need, and set limits
on the scope of your design.

1   *Who is the intranet for and what will it contain?* It is important to consider
    how the intranet will be used. Is it aimed exclusively at journalists or
    will it be used by your department as well? An intranet can be a useful
    tool for librarians as well as a means of supplying information to
    others. Are you looking for a platform for existing databases, or do you
    want to roll out timelines, factboxes and weblinks? Will you give users

access to subscription services, or keep them within the library? There are many valid uses for an intranet and you should consider all of them, whether you include them in your final design or not.

2   *Who will design and maintain the intranet?* You need to work out who will be tasked with designing and maintaining the intranet. It is important for library staff to be involved from the beginning, but will one person take on the role of editor or will the entire office team be involved? Maintenance can be a time-consuming task and it is vital to ensure you have the resources to cope, particularly if there will be no full-time intranet manager. Be realistic about the amount of time the library can dedicate to updating the intranet, as this will dictate its scope and size. Designate a project manager to oversee the work, but remember to keep other staff members in the loop; even if they won't be directly involved, they will be regular intranet users and can keep a look-out for new resources.

3   *Do you have outside support?* It is vital for the library to have support from other departments in your company, including the IT department. If your IT department already runs a company-wide intranet, the staff should be happy to offer support but, if not, will you be able to rely on them for back-up or will you need to employ an outside company? You also need backing from managers; the decision-makers need to be supportive of the project if your intranet is to remain a priority.

4   *Do your users want it?* Before you start to design an intranet you must ensure that there is a market for it. If no one is going to use your resource then you have wasted your time. The best way of assessing your internal market is to speak to potential users directly. If you can find out what they want from an intranet and, just as importantly, what they don't want, then you can design a system that will be practical and widely used. You can also learn from peers who have designed their own intranets, read articles about intranet design (including those listed at the end of this chapter) and contact other media libraries to find out about their experiences.

5   *Who is your audience?* Identify groups of key users who would benefit from your intranet. Start by drawing up a list of the main departments that use your enquiry service. Most of your users are probably journalists, but think beyond the obvious: the intranet at the Daily Mail is used heavily by the advertising department, for example, and the ResearchNet events diary is used by newsdesk administrators. Don't forget internal

use either. Your intranet could be a great way of disseminating and storing information for your own department.

Next steps

1   *Create a focus group.* A focus group is a great way of honing your intranet. Initially the group can brainstorm design and content ideas. Later on, they can provide vital feedback on mock-ups and redesigns before you launch the final product. Make sure you include people from different backgrounds, including library staff, journalists and technical support staff who know about software and hardware. Find out if anyone else from within the company has experience of creating an intranet as they could provide useful input.

2   *Speak to users.* One way of finding out what users want from an intranet is to design a questionnaire. This is a good way of asking specific questions and if you limit its length you are likely to get a decent number of replies. You may find, however, that some users, journalists in particular, say they don't have time to fill it in, which may skew or limit the results. An alternative is to identify users sympathetic to the library and speak to them directly. This way you can gain input from all user groups and a short questionnaire e-mailed to specific people is more likely to get a good response than a longer survey sent to all staff. Remember that users may have no experience of intranets, so you may need to mock up a simple version to show them what's possible. If you do not have time to create a questionnaire then an informal chat with chosen users can give you good ideas.

3   *Monitor queries.* If you find that users do not respond to a questionnaire, or are unwilling to discuss intranets, you could monitor general queries that come through the library. Keeping track of enquiries for a month will provide you with a good overview of the resources that are most in demand. It will also help you identify services that can be rolled out to users, such as telephone directories or *Encyclopaedia Britannica*, and spot areas that would save the library time and effort if they were online. For example, if you find you compile a lot of country profiles, then storing them all on the intranet would mean you would not have to start from scratch, compiling from disparate sources every time you receive a request. Monitoring will also give you a better idea of which departments use you the most and are therefore your intranet's key audience.

4   *Conduct an information audit.* Assessing your department's resources can help you identify what could be placed on the intranet. If your budget can stretch to it, you could design the intranet as a portal for online subscription services like Know UK, Red Pages and 192.com. You could also use the intranet to provide users with library databases such as a book catalogue or a list of cuttings files. An audit will provide you with a comprehensive list of the library's resources.

5   *Benchmark against your peers.* Comparing intranet ideas with other media librarians is a great way of discovering what has worked for others and what has not. This is true whether you are designing your department's first intranet or redesigning an existing system. Speak to librarians at social events organized by professional associations (such as, in the UK, AUKML, the Association of UK Media Librarians) or ask to visit and look at their intranet. There is no point repeating the same mistakes as your peers. Instead, learn from them and use their experiences in your own design.

6   *Trust your expertise.* It is true that you should not second-guess your users and assume you know what they will want from an intranet, but do not feel you have to include absolutely everything that they suggest either. It is you who will have to maintain the intranet so, if their suggestions are unworkable, then leave them out. An investigative journalist may want access to Factiva, but subscriptions are expensive and your budget may be limited. Someone who is used to accessing Hansard through a weblink directory might demand that you keep it, but these days it is just as easy to find Hansard reports through Google, and link directories are high-maintenance. Sometimes you will know best.

Intranet content
Choosing your content

What you include in your intranet will have a big impact on its usability and functionality and it is equally important what you exclude as include. You need to tailor it to the specific needs of your company and avoid overburdening users with unnecessary features, making it hard for them to locate what they really need. You must be able to maintain all the content you provide, as an intranet with out-of-date information is worse than useless.

1   *Existing online content.* Assess what already exists electronically and can
    be incorporated into the new intranet. You can build features from an older
    version of an intranet or from online databases into your new intranet.
    Their existing users will also constitute a ready-made client base.

2   *Scope.* An intranet must be manageable. You should consider all the
    possible uses for your intranet but what you include will depend on time
    and budget limitations. Some libraries, such as the one at the *Guardian*,
    only include content grown and managed by their own department on
    their intranet pages. Others, such as News International (Figure 2.3),
    manage content for the entire company intranet, giving them a high profile
    within the organization, but restricting the time they dedicate to updating

Figure 2.3   The News International intranet front page

the specific library resources. Decide early on whether your intranet is a portal to other resources or if it consists of data compiled by the library. This will be dictated by how much time you have to dedicate to managing the content, how many services you subscribe to and how many of these services you can afford to roll out company-wide.

3   *Topical vs historical.* Whether your intranet is a current awareness resource or historical archive of data will depend on the amount of time you and your team has to dedicate to updating content. Providing topical, up-to-date information draws users in and promotes the library. You can e-mail news editors with a link to the intranet when you add a new factsheet on an upcoming event. In early 2007 a member of the *Guardian* Research and Information Team compiled a page of resources on the Falklands War, which was used heavily by journalists compiling 25th anniversary reports (Figure 2.4). However, a topical intranet requires a proactive team, which can be a difficult adjustment for

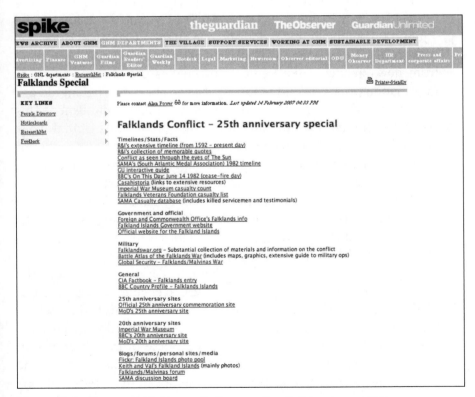

Figure 2.4   ResearchNet compilation on the Falklands conflict

librarians accustomed to responding to journalist requests. You may find you encounter resistance from colleagues who think they know what journalists want but are unable to produce any evidence, but it is worth persevering. Another problem is that topical data must be updated regularly, a problem for libraries without a team dedicated to running the intranet. An alternative is using your intranet to store historical data already compiled by the library. Historical content can be valuable. The cyclical nature of news means it is useful to recall old data when it becomes newsworthy once again, rather than having to research the issues from scratch. It is also useful to have a record of data and resources from the time for anniversaries of major news events. ResearchNet combines both approaches. It contains an archive of old factboxes and chronologies that are no longer updated but is also regularly refreshed with current news specials, accessed through the front page, on Iraq, Afghanistan, the Middle East and other key news areas. The library also provides ongoing chronologies of stand-alone news events updated as they happen, such as a day-by-day timeline following the 7 July 2005 bombings in London and one on the aftermath of Hurricane Katrina in the USA. This original data adds value to commercial data from news agencies like Reuters and makes the library central to information provision and reporting. Newspaper libraries should ask for a byline whenever intranet data they compiled is published. This raises the library's profile and gives due credit for original work (something journalists recognize but librarians are apt to take for granted). An instruction at the top of each page of any documents given to the enquirer will remind journalists and editors to credit you.

4   *Weblink pages*. When news intranets were originally designed in the 1990s, they were seen as an ideal platform for providing lists of URLs to useful websites. At the time, search engines were in their infancy so librarians could apply their professional skills to seeking out new pages and telling journalists about them. It is arguable that today the internet is sufficiently well mapped, and search engines so sophisticated, that most journalists are capable of searching the web themselves. Weblinks are very time-consuming because they need to be checked frequently to ensure they are still active. Some of the libraries that founded their intranet pages on libraries of weblinks, such as the library of Associated Newspapers, have abandoned those pages. At BBC

research.gateway they are certainly not the priority they were once considered. However, Sellors (2007) has noted that deep linking weblinks to subscription products within subject categories can increase their usage (for example, they have a 'Defence' category, which deep links to relevant titles from CredoReference and Oxford Reference Online). She has also found that sites listed at the top of the page are the most heavily used. Weblink pages may be a more useful tool in a larger organization covering a broader subject range than a daily newspaper, in which case categories should reflect subject divisions among production and journalistic staff.

5   *Niche content.* Niche content can be the hook on which you draw in new users. If you have unique resources that are not readily available on the web, for example cuttings files, books, magazines and online subscription, provide database access to them through your intranet. You can also compile content which others can access but lack the time to exploit. ResearchNet includes a future events diary compiled from disparate sources (newswires and Foresight News). Editors and journalists can access the wires themselves, and desk administrators have logons for Foresight News, but they have no time to search effectively for future events. They use the events diary to plan future spreads and spot upcoming anniversaries and events to be covered by the paper (Figure 2.5 on next page).

6   *Library-only areas.* Don't forget that the intranet is a tool for you as well as your users. Keeping a separate, restricted access area for internal library use can enable you to share information not of use outside the department. ResearchNet has several password-protected pages, containing information on how to update the intranet, personal contact details and 'how to' guides.

7   *Use reputable sources.* Everyone working for a media organization should use reputable research sources. This is vital when it comes to intranet content or your company risks being sued. Make sure that the information provided on every page is sourced so journalists know where it has come from. This means that if the data is queried you can refer to the original source.

8   *Updating.* Intranets must be manageable or they will become out of date and lose the library credibility. How much content you add to your intranet will be dictated by time limitations and whether you have a

dedicated team or librarians fit the work into their daily jobs. Assess your resources continuously and avoid information overload. Most libraries access a vast amount of data via their information resources, but you should resist the temptation to provide too much for your users. You should offer quality rather than quantity.

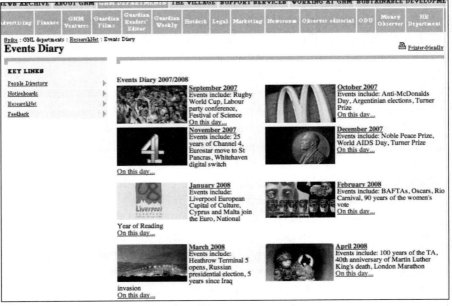

Figure 2.5   ResearchNet Events Diary

Designing your intranet

Once you have selected your intranet content you must decide how best to present it, allowing simple navigation and functionality. Intranet users need to find exactly what they need quickly and easily. A well designed site will attract users, but if they have a frustrating and time-consuming experience this will lead to low hit rates and negative word of mouth.

1   *Look to others for inspiration.* The wealth of good-quality websites already in existence means you don't have to look too hard for ideas. When ResearchNet relaunched, the main BBC page was an early template for its design. You should also look at your own company's website as retaining a familiar corporate style can ease navigation; for example, always have the search engine or 'contact us' in the same corner

as on the main site. The BBC's research.gateway is a good example of this, as on each page there is a helpful 'I want to . . .' section in the same location on each page, giving users clear guidance for locating the information they need (Figure 2.6).

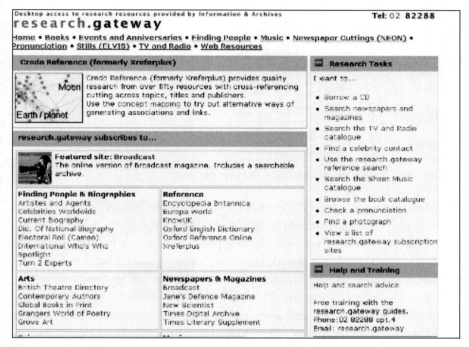

Figure 2.6   BBC research.gateway home page

2   *Follow basic principles.* First impressions count and a clean, well-structured site attracts users. Sections and subject headings should be clearly defined and unambiguous. Avoid library jargon or any other unfamiliar terminology. Users want to scan the front page quickly, recognize the resource they require and retrieve information in as few clicks as possible. When News International relaunched News Cast, its confusing and cluttered design led to the library's most useful content being buried, increasing the click rate and the users' frustration (Figure 2.7 on next page). Routine enquiries to the library increased, as users called simply to find information they had previously been able to find on their own.

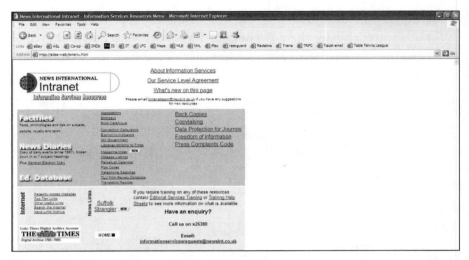

Figure 2.7   News International's library intranet

3 *Stamp your authority.* The intranet should state its library ownership and
   reflect its professionalism in terms of content and style. Add credibility
   by demonstrating that there is a real, physical presence behind the virtual
   resource. Displaying up-to-date and correct contact information lets
   users know whom to contact if they have queries or feedback about the
   site. The *Herald*'s intranet Dookit is a great example, effectively sign-
   posting the content but also making the library's involvement clear
   (Figure 2.8 on next page). If an intranet provides links to external sources or organizations you should ensure these are credible and authoritative,
   and that links are regularly checked. Make sure all your content is sourced
   correctly and clearly, avoid typographical errors and update frequently.

4 *Choose good simple design and easy finding aids.* Flash technology or
   scrolling images may be seen as a good way to enliven a site but users
   often find such tools gimmicky and distracting. However, pictures
   break up chunks of text which might overwhelm users and can
   highlight desirable features. One of ResearchNet's most useful and
   popular resources is its diary of events and anniversaries. To draw
   attention to it we use four photographs to highlight certain upcoming
   events and we also use pictures to represent our 'exclusive access'
   products Who's Who and OED. Site maps and search engines are
   excellent tools for helping users navigate sites quickly and effectively.
   Associated Newspapers' library's intranet E-Lib is essentially a portal

Figure 2.8   Dookit, the Herald's library intranet

using a federated search. In one click a user can search the library's text and picture archive as well as the internet and other databases. The lack of browsable content makes E-Lib simple, clean and uniform, but it also relies on users knowing exactly what they are looking for (Figure 2.9 on next page).

Testing your design

Prototyping and testing formats are critical aspects of intranet design. ResearchNet's initial design ideas consisted of paper drawings submitted to members of the research department and the Spike team. Feedback and consultation ensued followed by more designs, feedback and consultation before any electronic prototype appeared. Staff had intensive training on a number of applications to create intranet page mock-ups and the final design for ResearchNet. If your department is taking responsibility for the day-to-day running of your intranet you may need training. You will also need to consult your IT department to ensure the intranet works on all your users' servers and browsers.

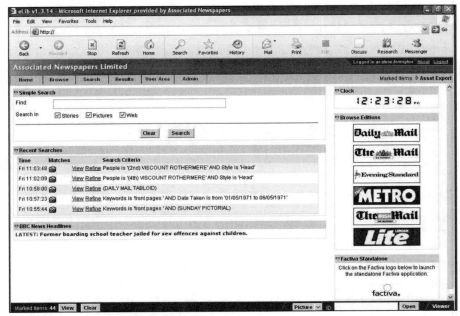

Figure 2.9 Associated Newspapers' intranet E-Lib

Ideally, designs should be tested on your target audience for feedback or suggestions. Surveys, focus groups or one-to-one sessions with users can elicit crucial design ideas which you or your team had previously failed to consider. Even testing with a just a few users will be beneficial. In fact research by Jakob Nielsen (Nielsen, 2000) found the best results came from small tests involving no more than five users. Before the BBC relaunched its intranet in 2005 it carried out intensive user-testing across the organization, as did the research.gateway team responsible for the research pages. Both resources have scored highly with users because their designs work so effectively. Involving users also gives them a sense of emotional investment and increases anticipation for the final product.

Marketing

A new or revamped intranet needs an effective marketing strategy to ensure it not only launches successfully but also retains users in the future. There are many channels and tools which can employed. The scale of promotion will be determined by your available budget and resources but tailoring your marketing to your target audience is essential if your intranet has any chance of success.

Developing a strategy

Identifying your audience is the foundation of marketing an intranet. If you have carried out user surveys or testing during the design stage you will already know who your users are and what kind of information they are looking for. Knowing your users means you can anticipate how they might respond to different means of promotion. You can also identify different types of users and target them with relevant features or resources.

Hard and soft launches

Departments with a large marketing budget may choose a hard launch, a large-scale event which may involve a party or company presentation. This can create a high level of expectation but many in media organizations have become wary of endless, much-trumpeted launches of initiatives or resources by other sections of their companies. Many libraries, including those at the *Guardian*, the *Herald* and Associated Newspapers, opted instead for a soft launch, a more low key approach using certain marketing tools, but also relying on word of mouth. Instead of a blanket approach, users are targeted more directly based on their individual needs.

Marketing tools

1 *Ask the experts*. Use the expertise available to you from your organization's internal communications or marketing departments. Whoever runs your company intranet can tell you how they launched and continue to market their site. The company intranet itself is an excellent place to promote the library's intranet. It can be used to announce the launch and, as with research.gateway on the BBC's gateway intranet, provide a permanent and prominent access point to the intranet (Figure 2.10 on next page). You could also ask your IT department about loading your intranet as users' home page or automatically adding it to their bookmarks.

2 *Use existing communication channels*. If your library has a newsletter or noticeboard make sure it includes details about the new intranet. Send e-mail alerts or, if your organization has electronic noticeboards or bulletin boards, use them to promote new resources. Embed URLs into posts so users can link directly to the relevant page. RSS feeds are another excellent device for keeping users informed of new additions to your intranet. Library managers should use head of department meetings

Figure 2.10 BBC gateway intranet home page

to inform other managers about the intranet. Staff who carry out enquiry work can also promote the intranet to users with whom they come into contact, for example by directing customers to the appropriate section of the site rather than simply answering the question using the same research tool. This depends on your colleagues buying into the notion of the intranet, so it is important to make sure they are properly informed. The email signatures of all library staff should also include a link to the new intranet.

3 *Brochures and handouts.* You should provide users with simple documents outlining the intranet's key features and benefits, to take away and keep for future reference. The BBC's research.gateway team distributes well-produced help sheets for presentations and training. Your organization's graphics or design department could help you in producing a professional brochure featuring corporate branding.

4 *Intranet name.* Having an eyecatching and memorable intranet name is

important to give it an identity. Running a naming competition before launching the intranet not only promotes it but makes users feel involved, generating a sense of ownership, a device used by the *Herald* when they launched their new intranet 'Dookit'. A distinctive logo is also a good way of creating an identity.

5   *Merchandise.* If you have the budget, branded merchandise such as pens, mouse mats or Post-it notes can be very effective. Make sure they clearly show the intranet's name and logo as well as the URL or a telephone contact number.

6   *Induction sessions and training.* Experience has shown media libraries that the most effective marketing tool is one-to-one contact with users. Group presentations may seem like a good idea but they are difficult to facilitate and attendance is usually low. Make sure the library and intranet are included in staff inductions, which will promote both your site and the wider department. You could also target new starters directly by e-mail. Journalists tend to cite lack of time as a reason for not attending events such as intranet demonstrations and a quick and tailored demonstration at their desk is an effective alternative. The BBC's research.gateway team have also found that many journalists are put off by the word 'training' and that 'troubleshooting' sessions elicit a more positive response. Associated Newspapers trained 'super-users' from each department, hoping the skills would cascade down to colleagues and staff. Unfortunately 'super-users' were too busy to pass on skills or even to attend the initial session. The staff also placed user guides online but concluded that one-to-one training at a user's desk is the most powerful way of recruiting converts. Finally, construct your training sessions to highlight relevant features to the trainee. For example, ResearchNet's events diary features prominently in training sessions for desk administrators who plan journalists' diaries.

7   *Word of mouth.* If a user is impressed with a new product it is likely they will recommend it to others. This is particularly effective when they are in a position of authority and influence and you should target such people directly. Choose a regular library user who would be happy to promote your intranet and may even provide a testimonial for your site or promotional literature. Every interaction you or your colleagues have with users is an easy, free-of-charge opportunity to market your intranet. Marketing does not end with the launch. It is a continuous

process, ensuring all users, new and existing, are aware of your intranet and its benefits.

Managing your intranet

Once your intranet project is complete and the site is launched, you are on your own. It is crucial that your new intranet is sustainable. This requires putting into place appropriate structures and procedures, as discussed below.

1   *Provide a framework.* You should have comprehensive documentation outlining the objectives of the intranet and providing clear guidance as to how it will be maintained. A statement of mission and aims will provide current and future intranet editors with a point of reference to ensure they are continuing to meet the original remit.

2   *Allocate resources.* It is essential to determine who will be responsible for the day-to-day running of your site and what tools and support they will need. Most libraries do not have a budget for intranet development or a full-time intranet manager. At the BBC there are four dedicated members of staff in charge of creating and maintaining content on the research.gateway intranet, in addition to an enquiries service, which is funded separately. Two people are responsible for the events diary, which is seen as a key feature of the site. The library at Associated Newspapers is dedicated entirely to its intranet E-Lib site, working proactively on maintaining text and picture databases and managing subscriptions. For Associated Newspapers' users E-lib encompasses the library. In other libraries, such as those at the *Guardian* and News International, one member of staff has overall responsibility for the intranet in addition to their ordinary duties. Other members of staff are equipped to do routine updating to cover absences and, at the *Guardian*, they have a deputy editor. At the *Herald* daily updating duties are incorporated into the staff rota to ensure that content is always current. Within a busy media library it is important to put procedures in place so the site does not become out of date. Time allocated will vary: at the *Herald* the team can spend up to three hours a day updating Dookit, while at the *Guardian* an hour a day is more usual.

3   **Provide support tools**. Intranet editors should have relevant training and documentation such as online training manuals. A style guide is essential for those writing content for the intranet. Not only is writing

for the web very different from writing in print, it is important that web pages reflect the format of the intranet and the conventions of the organization as a whole.

4   *Manage time and expectations.* The more content and features you add to your intranet the more you have to maintain. Media libraries often have limited time and resources making it difficult to keep a large database of links, timelines and so on up to date in the ever-changing news environment. It is best to concentrate on a manageable number of key features than try to cover every possible area. Hit rates and usage statistics can help you identify which resources are the most popular and the most important to focus on and develop. Underused resources could either be marketed more aggressively or dropped to make room for something else. Losing unpopular resources can tailor the intranet more effectively and possibly save money.

5   *Keep it fresh.* Without new content an intranet quickly stagnates so you should always look for new ideas. Keep informed about news about your organization as well as general current affairs, and keep up to date with changes on the company's main intranet that may benefit your pages. Seek feedback from your users to see what works, what does not and what else they would like to see on the intranet. Encourage your immediate colleagues to suggest ways of improving content and keep informed about what other media libraries are doing. Keep abreast of developments in intranet technology. Wikis, blogs and RSS feeds can be useful additions to your intranet, attracting new users and encouraging feedback and discussion. Remember to inform users of changes or additions to content.

6   *Ongoing support.* Managing your intranet successfully also depends on receiving an adequate amount of commitment from senior management and colleagues. Management support can help secure the resources and time you need successfully to maintain your intranet. The intranet should be a priority within your department and have backing from the whole team. If colleagues are to be involved in updating content it is necessary that they are convinced the resource is worth investing their time in. Make sure you maintain the inter-departmental relationships you created during the initial project. Your IT department should be able to assist in any technical issues in the future and you should be aware of any developments affecting internal communications in your

organization. Try and be involved if there is a cross-departmental working group or consultation process looking at intranets.

The future for media librarians and intranets

The future of intranets in media libraries is intrinsically linked to the future of media libraries themselves. As information becomes increasingly available online, it may be that the intranet will become the library for many users. Media librarians become gatekeepers to information resources, rolling them out to users, and the intranet their portal or access point. This does not mean an intranet should replace media librarians. A well managed and promoted intranet can enhance the library's role as a proactive provider of topical information rather than a depository of old cuttings files. Traditional librarians' skills are perfectly suited and, indeed, essential to uploading, managing and promoting the content which makes a successful intranet.

Changes to many media organizations' working practices also increase the importance of having an efficient library intranet. Although news publishers and broadcasters anticipate 24/7 working, library headcount and opening hours have in most cases been cut. Staff with remote access and working flexibly need a constantly updated, easily accessible and topical intranet more than ever. When physical library services are unavailable the library presence and role can be maintained through the intranet. Media librarians must see intranets as an opportunity rather than a threat. Giving users access to information sources will never replace the value-added research provided by librarians, but it can reduce routine enquiries and enable librarians to concentrate on more complex research.

The authors' overriding conclusion from their research is that effectively managed, well designed and successfully marketed intranets can have a positive impact on a media library's status within its organization. However, this can only be achieved by involving all your stakeholders, especially your potential users, at every stage of the intranet's development. Ultimately your users will be the judges who determine the fate of your intranet. Making them the focus of all planning, consultation, testing and marketing will undoubtedly help you achieve your goals.

Acknowledgements

With thanks to: Lindsey Sellors (BBC), Catherine Watson (*Herald*), Gertrud

Erbach and Mark Sumner (News International), Steve Torrington (Associated Newspapers) and Richard Nelsson and Caroline White (*Guardian* News and Media).

References

Nielsen, J. (2000) Why You Only Need to Test With Five Users, *Alertbox*, (29 March), www.useit.com/alertbox/20000319.html.

Sellors, L. (2007) Personal communication (31 October).

White, M. (1998) Intranet Resources on the Web, *Freepint*, (30 April), www.freepint.com/issues/300498.htm.

Chapter 3

Picture libraries and librarianship

GRAEME BOYD

Most forms of published media use still images to add value to, illustrate or break up spoken or written words. The number of images used has increased in the past few years because of technological possibilities and commercial pressures. Even radio programmes now often run websites illustrated by pictures associated with their broadcasts. The ever-expanding number of platforms for images has made media organizations hungry for new sources. Many media organizations run their own picture archives and, bucking the early 1990s trend for disposing of in-house resources, are finding them profitable sources of income, especially if they have invested in a sales infrastructure or e-commerce platform. Other media organizations rely on external sources of pictures, notably photographic agencies, libraries and archives, which either represent their own unique collections or are mediators for other people's photographs. The range of collections useful for publication may cover not just photographs, but engravings, manuscripts and lithographs.

This chapter takes an overview of picture collections, how they can be used by picture researchers and the issues that emerge for those managing picture collections. Questions concerning managing collections are largely dealt with in the earlier part of the chapter and the role of the picture librarian in the second part. The author is particularly interested in giving a taste of the picture library world for those new to the profession or considering entering it. Although it is primarily aimed at picture librarians who work for media organizations, those in that position may identify themselves more with the wider picture library community than with the other kinds of information professional within the media or even within their own organization. The author, who currently manages both still and moving images run by the environmental charity Greenpeace, has worked in a range of areas, from a picture collection at fashion magazine publisher Condé Nast, to an information research unit at the BBC, to the library at the Glasgow School of Art. This gives him a unique insight into the common ground shared between librarians working in the media industry and those working in other fields, but also the ability to identify the picture-related issues which concern media librarians in particular.

Picture libraries and their customers

At the time of writing, two acquisitive multinational picture agencies, Getty and Corbis, dominate the commercial picture industry. They emerged in the 1990s to transform the crusty, dusty picture archive industry into a digital 20th-century industry. They carry out a hard-fought battle for control of the image market, buying up the intellectual property rights of picture collections and generating huge profits as a result. After Corbis bought the Bettmann Archive in 1995 and Getty the Tony Stone and Hulton Archive a few years later, no other agency has matched their scale. Were they to merge, it would seem the whole of visual history could one day be controlled through a single enterprise.

However, aside from these two giants, picture libraries vary in their specializations and sizes. Some libraries deal with a single subject or photographer while others cover the generality of subjects, but each has a distinctive selling point. Stock libraries are the most common form of picture archive and act as a convenient source of images to fill brochures, leaflets and flyers. Good stock libraries keep in tune with current trends and regularly replace stock. Other libraries include archival libraries, commercial libraries and libraries specializing by subject, in anything from art to zoology. Most organizations which publish newspapers, magazines and television programmes have their own internal picture libraries, which enable journalists and production staff to find the image they need quickly and easily against tight deadlines. Keeping an in-house store of images is a cost-effective alternative to commissioning new photographs every time they require a picture. There is also currently a steady growth in small picture libraries offering a niche, personalized service, specializing in a particular subject such as news, culture, social history or food and drink.

Picture library customers include an array of creative businesses including film and television companies, PR and marketing agencies, newspapers and magazines. Many relish the chance to work with picture agency staff who are experts in their field and who, at their most skilled, effectively act as a consultancy service for them. Some inexperienced researchers and journalists are unaware of the kind of help a picture library can give and, intimidated by face-to-face transactions, retreat to using e-commerce picture websites or even illegally downloading poor-quality images from the web. As they do not know about images they are missing, they perpetuate the existence of poor-quality or repetitive photographic illustration in the media. Luckily they are by no means the only picture archive customers.

Commercial picture libraries survive by predicting their customers' needs. If someone calls requesting a specific image the library does not have, then a sales opportunity is lost. Successful picture libraries anticipate needs, often developing different collections for a specific community or market. Staff need to monitor how images are being used in the media, in order to predict and understand the visual landscape, and keep track of what customers are buying and why. Customers may be far away, as the picture library industry increasingly relies on foreign markets, many using overseas agents and outlets to build relationships, and internet sales have increased the scope for picture libraries to operate outside their home territory. Jane Hance, a picture industry professional with 12 years' experience, says that it is important:

> to understand the markets you are providing images to. Whether it's publishing, advertising or corporate. It's a real advantage to thoroughly understand the type of images the client is looking for. The photos should always be fit for the purpose. For example you don't need advertising photographers to shoot for educational books. Images have to be reflected in the text, they have to do the talking. Finally, remember you are providing a service.

Copyright and licensing

Photographers retain the rights over the images they create, but they license picture archives or agencies to represent their work, normally exclusively over an agreed period of time. A typical deal would give the photographer a fixed percentage whenever the library sells one of their images. It is part of the picture librarian's role to protect copyright and make sure they do not infringe someone else's rights. UK copyright law states that original work is copyright-protected as soon as it has been recorded in any way, whether on paper, in an audio recording, on film or electronically. In addition to rights-protected images, some picture agencies offer royalty-free pictures, where the customer pays a flat fee for unlimited usage.

Picture researchers often have trouble convincing the creative community that having an image in their possession does not make it theirs to use as they wish. Those working outside picture archives can be pressurized to use an image whose provenance is in doubt. It is good practice to keep a paper trail of their efforts in trying to establish the source of an image, to prove that every possible effort was made to try and trace the original copyright-holder should a dispute emerge. Journalists are sometimes also presented with free pictures from non-picture-library sources, such as tourist offices or public relations companies. These often are not really 'free' because the time expended to obtain them is disproportionate to the fee saved by going to a picture library from the outset.

Copyright in an image exists in the UK for 70 years after the death of the author, but the intricacies of copyright law mean this is not always straightforward. There may, for example, be specific sales embargos on an image. The author has worked with photographers and photographers' agents who require written details about researchers requesting to use their work before they will grant access. Picture libraries must adhere to such requests to uphold the reputation of the archive and make sure they are trusted with photographers' work in the future.

A model release form should always be signed if an image to be used for commercial gain (such as in an advertisement) has a picture of a person in it (this is designated 'commercial' rather than 'editorial' use). The form is likely to state that the person or persons photographed have consented to this and to have their image reproduced. However, it is often obtained after the event and the subject may feel they are being exploited once they know there might be profit involved or have personal objections to the context in which it is going to be used. For editorial use, pictures do not normally need to be 'model released', although in extreme circumstances it could be advisable, for example if an image is used to depict an illegal or distasteful activity.

Digital copyright

Copyright law is still catching up with the potential released by developments in visual technology. It is unclear, for example, who owns the copyright of a new image that has been created from two or more other images. Even where the law is clear, however, preventing the illegal downloading of photographs from websites is difficult.

Digital watermarking or 'fingerprinting' is one means picture agencies have for preventing pictures from being used before or even after purchase. A translucent logo or virtually imperceptible code is embedded into a digital image to identify ownership, encoded so that it does not show, cannot be deliberately removed or tampered with (cropped or distorted) and is still there when a picture is altered, when only part of it is used and when it crosses different media, for example from a digital scan to a print medium and back again. However, it is expensive, still in its infancy, and many smaller libraries choose to invest in other areas. Others will make an image available before purchase with a visible watermark, but once the client has paid for and downloaded a clean, high-quality image, the library is powerless to prevent the client using it again, other than with legal action after publication.

Pricing

The prices picture libraries charge to license images to their customers depend on how they are used and on market trends and practices, such as print runs, exposure and syndication. The nature of the image does not affect the price. Customers purchasing images for commercial use pay more than if they purchase for editorial use. Most libraries will negotiate on price, as it is always beneficial to have pictures used and be credited as the source, and offer deals for regular users and those buying in bulk. If clients wish to use the image for a purpose beyond the original licence, such as for foreign or new editions of books, or the extension of an advertising campaign by time or territory, further permission is required. It is rare, however, that clients license an image for use in a single country; most require and pay for world rights. Pricing is a delicate operation and the average photographer would not know how to cost an image fee. Occasionally new agencies emerge promising a greater percentage to the photographer, but they rarely survive commercially. Photographers and picture libraries rely on each other to ensure that a healthy market for images survives.

Digital photographs
The arrival of the internet

The internet has revolutionized the picture library industry from many different points of view. First, the traditional purchasers for images, those who publish books, magazines and newspapers or make advertisements, have expanded into the digital world, requiring more images to fill up this new space. Second, many picture libraries have digitized some or all of their image collections and made them available online. In most cases, they have found new clients and markets who either were not aware of their holdings or were not tempted to buy until they could do so via e-commerce, particularly if they were based in a different country from the picture archive.

Electronic delivery has massively increased the speed with which images can be passed from owner to customer and, beyond that, processed for publication. Jane Hance remarks:

> The industry has changed so much since I first started. Agencies all used to work with transparencies and we would send out piles of transparencies to clients. Clients used to check off on delivery notes that all were received and had to ensure that all were returned. This is the biggest change, as this administrative task was so time consuming and so many transparencies would go missing with huge loss fees to pay. This also meant all deadlines were dependent on the post and so things could take a few days to arrive, a huge difference in terms of picture deadlines. Selections had to all take place at light boxes and there was very little photo manipulation that took place. With digital there is less administration, no loss fees and no waiting for post!

Moreover, as documentary photographer Robert Knoth believes, 'digital picture quality is constantly improving and will eventually match the quality of photographic film'.

Hard copy vs digital

Digital images are not without problems, however. Many publishers still select from transparencies rather than digital images for quality control reasons, mainly regarding the regulation of colour. A researcher can select a transparency using a lightbox and the human eye. If the colour contrast or colour saturation within a digital image is changed, quality is lost, leaving little room for adjustment. Sometimes problems only appear after a digital image has been blown up. A researcher selecting a digital thumbnail may be unaware that it has been poorly scanned or saved in the wrong resolution or format until they see it at its full size, by which time they will have wasted effort and money.

Once a print has been digitized, it can be reproduced endlessly with no harm to the original. This has left many libraries with the question of whether they should pay to store the original image. Some argue that the original print has acquired integrity and artefactual value throughout its life. Has it not changed colour, shape and smell? Does it not offer historic, artistic and financial value? They would argue that scanning an image simply freezes a moment in its history (and in the history of technological development). A scan of an ancient lithograph is not the same as holding it in one's hand.

As it stands, the industry is in a hybrid state; it is partly physical, but mostly digital, at least at the point of delivery if not of long-term storage. Picture libraries still deal with a full spectrum of clients, from those who regularly download images to those who prefer to spend hours inspecting transparencies over a photo lightbox. The latter are aware that only a small number of the world's images are available online. Moreover, the conglomeration of previously independent pictures sources has made it more difficult to find unseen, unusual images which can be part of the thrill for the researcher. These loyal users, normally working in publishing, will always enjoy the tactile familiarity of selecting material and physically leafing through portfolios. They are happiest being lost in a basement of wall-to-wall filing cabinets full of negatives, prints and transparencies.

Libraries are by nature user-friendly and the best picture librarians, if they can, encourage personal visits. This is because, in the author's experience, it is very difficult to interpret from the client exactly what they are looking for through a phone call or an e-mail, particularly with images representing intangible concepts like 'happiness' or 'teamwork'. Often the client knows exactly what they have in mind but needs to browse through a range of images before they can articulate it. Another advantage of a personal visit is that seeing unexpected pictures may spark off new ideas. Moreover, an image is more likely to be used if the client selects it personally.

For libraries, the main disadvantage of clients' physical contact with their collections is the inevitable deterioration of the pictures' condition. As Nick Galvin from Magnum Photos believes:

> the more digitisation that happens, the more valuable these physical archives will become. At Magnum around two-fifths of our images are scanned and online. These will be within the subjects that we have most requests for, the most popular subjects or persons. It is a viable commercial decision as to what has not to be scanned. Commercial pressures mean we offer online material first. Only if it was a large book project we were doing, would we use the originals.

Digitizing collections

Library staff need only basic ICT experience to clean, retouch or reposition a hardcopy image in a scanning machine. Unfortunately this is time-consuming, labour-intensive and expensive, as it can take anything up to an hour to prepare and scan a picture depending on the speed and quality of the machine.

The investment required for large-scale digitization projects is daunting, not just in technological equipment, training and time, but also in the level of sustained marketing and advertising needed to let existing and new customers know they can now access your collection online. Linda Royles from the British Association of Picture Libraries & Agencies (BAPLA) believes that 'whilst costs of producing, storing and distributing digital images is cheaper in some ways than working with analogue, investment in technology to convert from analogue to digital and to have a client-focused searchable site is expensive'. Moreover, expert decision-making is needed to select which materials should be digitized, for how long and what kind of technical infrastructure will be needed to support the vast number of formats, not to mention whether the original is kept and how many copies if so.

However, the advantages can pay lucrative rewards. Robert Elwall from the Royal Institute of British Architects (RIBA) notes 'For us, digitisation is primarily about access and facilitating the making available of our material in a wide range of forms. The adage of "digitise once, use many times" is certainly one of our driving forces and allows us to make our collection better known to a wider audience.'

Digital asset management systems

Acquiring a digital asset management (DAM) system allows picture librarians to identify, store, manage and retrieve 'media assets', normally still or moving images. A simple, user-friendly system can allow non-information professionals to enter basic picture information at the point the image is created. John Novis, picture editor at Greenpeace International, explains:

> We try and have our photographers do as much of the data input as they can whilst on the job. It's in their contract. We want them to concentrate on taking photos sure, but when they come to transmit us the images, usually over FTP [File Transfer Protocol] they should be able to deliver tagged images, with date, location, subject and notes direct in to the correct folder on our DAM system. When our cataloguer picks them up all they need to do is double check everything and add other key fields to make the images searchable and compliable internally.

Marketing and sales representatives from the software companies who make them (examples worth looking at include Orange Logic, Picdar and Virage) offer convincing evidence that picture libraries cannot survive without a DAM system. However, it is important to remember that it represents a continuing investment and archives should ask themselves whether their clients require a system before making the decision to purchase. They should compare prices on software and servicing before they look at products and speak to existing users to find out common faults and complaints about the product or service.

Metadata

As with any software that allows text to be stored and searched, the backbone of a DAM system is metadata, which allows the researcher to find images through words structured into categories. Without detailed image metadata, search options might be limited to freetext, file size, file format, colour or black and white. The potential for accurate searching can be enhanced when a subject field accesses a controlled language (also known as a taxonomy). Silver Oliver, BBC Information Architect, says: 'Now recent websites contain disambiguation software whereby the search engine can differentiate between identical words with different meanings: for example, orange the fruit, orange the colour and Orange the company.' The advantages of metadata use are not restricted to making searches more accurate. According to Oliver, 'By structuring your data using an established metadata standard you open up opportunities for sharing and processing resources between archives. Established metadata standards, like METS [the Metadata Encoding and Transmission Standard], are invaluable for developing preservation strategies and migrating between technologies.' He also highlights the importance of metadata in enabling media assets to be accessible in the long term:

> It is a commonly held belief that preservation is not a concern of born-digital objects. The medium of storage is as a rule relatively non-perishable. The opposite is, in fact, true due to the rapid obsolescence of standards for storing and accessing data. A great deal of thought must go into a preservation strategy to ensure a particular resource will be accessible in ten or even five years time. The foundation of a good preservation strategy is built on established metadata standards.

Standards and formats

Agreed format and content standards in picture libraries are necessary so that pictures can be shared with users and processed using their own production software. Today clients expect to use images in a variety of secondary multimedia products, from a clip on the internet, to incorporation within a video game, to a variety of DVDs and CD-ROMs. However, businesses continue to acquire software which does not support the formats in which digital files are held and no efforts are being made to ensure consistency across the industry. Admittedly, technological innovation can be frustrated by overly prescriptive standards, but it would certainly be a boon to the picture industry to minimize the plethora of file formats currently available. Unfortunately, information about standards is currently only documented by organizations that identify and promote them, not by a wider body which oversees and controls these organizations. An exception is BAPLA, which has been working with agencies and their clients on standards for image distribution and guidelines for standards of digitization.

Preservation

There is a very different approach needed for digital preservation than for traditional preservation. Some old photographs made with nitrate film can literally explode. Others suffer 'vinegar syndrome', decomposing and dissolving emitting a sour-smelling odour. A photograph left in the sun's full glare for an hour will fade, shrivel and curl. A good hard-copy storage strategy balances the need for customers and researchers to handle pictures with the need to keep them safe for future generations. Ideal conditions for long-term storage are a cool store where the temperature is kept at 15°C and relative humidity at 40%, backed up by freezer storage for at-risk acetate material.

However, stored carefully, we can look at images preserved on paper or glass negative 150 years after they were created. Digital information is evanescent and fragile and will not be accessible even in a few years if the software or hardware needed to access it is no longer available. Image formats pose even greater obsolescence problems than, say, word processing documents, because each format chooses to code the image in a different way. Essentially, traditions do not yet exist for digital material. Furthermore, digital storage offers the illusion that preservation is not a problem because, unlike analogue storage formats, a digital copy is ostensibly an exact replica of what was copied. This is not the case. Image formats degenerate, losing quality from the previous copy or 'generation'.

There is little leadership on the best way to preserve digital materials and hardly any standardization in formats. Picture archivists cannot predict the future of the digital assets they manage or who will want to access them; buying new technology takes precedence over funding preservation and the costs of providing current access often overlap with those for preservation. It could simply be that the pace at which new digital resources are being created is accelerating so quickly that no one has the time to think about anything else. Yet, to maximize the potential of picture archives' initial investment in digitization, preservation should be a priority and collaborative action is needed. Should we not be trying to improve the fragile, brittle longevity of film before we pick and mix which JPEG (Joint Photographic Experts Group), TIFF (Tagged Image File Format) or RAW file we save our high or low-resolution image on? Do we know how many original copies already exist of a digitized image? What will be historically and/or commercially valuable in the future? Public and private institutions should work together to preserve both traditional and digital images in the best way.

One solution might be a think tank or ideas store, made up of representatives of the national archives to assess the current preservation climate. Other positive action could be libraries sharing offsite storage facilities and using them co-operatively or different agencies dividing up responsibilities for specific services. The author is dismayed that large conglomerate agencies can buy up the market purely for content and no ruling body or auditor imposes terms that first stipulate their preservation strategy, past, present and future. Picture librarians should promote good practice, awareness-raising and training in digital preservation. They need to fulfil their traditional role as the custodians of the information of the future by collaborating to produce a clearly articulated vision of what is to happen to still images.

Qualities of a picture librarian

A modern picture librarian working for a small or medium-sized archive is likely to have a composite job, acting as part-librarian, part-archivist, part-curator, part-photographer and part-technology expert. Some of the qualities which might be needed and issues picture librarians meet in their working day are outlined below.

Main skills

The main skills for picture librarians are in:

- handling digital photographs
- handling and conserving hard copy
- publishing and controlling the quality of digital images (including colour management and screen calibration)
- meeting the needs of the publishing industry
- negotiating with clients
- meeting customers' needs
- researching and investigating
- basic ICT and database management.

Main competencies

The main competencies picture librarians require are:

- to work methodically
- resilience
- to pay attention to detail
- to be able to communicate.

Main activities

The main activities for picture librarians are:

- conducting research on behalf of clients
- responding to verbal descriptions with visual concepts
- negotiating fees
- negotiating deadlines
- writing licences or contracts
- compiling primary research.

Other activities

Other activities that picture librarians carry out are:

- responding to queries and giving advice on costs and rights
- discussing fees with clients
- dealing with contractual issues
- photographic research
- planning new departmental processes
- recruiting and training new staff and work experience
- setting up new procedures that will help the department run more smoothly.

Issues facing picture librarians
Disintermediation – picture research

Picture research was at one time a highly specialized activity carried out by skilled practitioners with minute knowledge of the holdings of the world's picture archives. Today a belief persists that most journalists and editors can search for pictures and conduct initial research themselves using the world wide web. Lacking the searching skills of trained professionals, most end-user searchers tend to rely heavily on browsing, so their searches cost more, take longer and are harder to filter to a concise end result. Their lack of knowledge of potential sources means they often rely on search engines like Google Images, which merely skim the surface, never penetrating the most valuable online picture archives, never mind those which have not been digitized. Moreover, web image searches calculate relevancy on the basis of text nearby to the image on a web page, which may or may not be accurate to the image. It remains the case that the highest-quality and most cost-effective research is carried out by qualified or trained picture researchers and librarians.

However, it is a challenge for picture researchers to sell their services and in-house picture libraries to justify their existence to their managers. The *Guardian*'s Information Manager Richard Nelsson describes, 'feeling like an information evangelist, proselytising the good word of the department, whether it's in a meeting or on the stairwell' (Nelsson, 2006). However, Head of Associated Press Archive Alwyn Lindsey believes:

> The expansion of online searching has not led to the demise of the professional researcher. Matching content to a creative brief requires skill for it to be done well. If you know that you need a specific image you can look for it online, but the issue is tougher when there's a vast quantity of material to sift through and that takes some skill and experience to find the best and most pertinent images. You have to be capable of making that judgement. Also, there are many instances where you need to match images to a concept where there is no specific image in mind, and this takes some creativity and lateral thinking on the part of a researcher.

By the time customers approach a library, 50% of the work should have been done. It is in the client's interest to give the clearest possible brief because prolonged research carried out by library staff often incurs a charge; even in-house collections may charge, even if you are part of the company. The archive should be provided with the anticipated size of reproduction, the size of the print run and the territories in which it will be distributed. Journalists and publishers expect ever more instantaneous results from picture libraries, and themselves often face tighter deadlines than in the pre-24-hour news age. However, fully interpreting the brief, preparing images and checking for copyright restrictions takes time and mistakes can be more costly in the long term.

Disintermediation – picture archiving

An increasing trend has been reducing staff in picture archives on the basis that the photographer can carry out part of their jobs. A handful of photographers are turning freelance to create their own independent online picture agencies. This bid for autonomy has been made possible by the ease of access and relative cheapness of the equipment needed. The prime motivation is to enable photographers to control their work and deal with clients directly, although predicted sales income must cover web design and maintenance costs. In 2007, 15% of the Corbis photographer workforce was cut on the basis that increasing numbers of images had become available on photographers' own websites. Their photographers, among the best in the business, now had to either build their own e-commerce websites and represent their own work or find another agency.

Photographer Robert Knoth believes: 'The cost and time for me to manage this [website] is a cost and a time which I should be using in taking pictures . . . . The Getties of this world have an infrastructure I cannot compete with. I need the global market to survive.' Nick Galvin from Magnum Photos, which acts as a 'co-operative' between photographer and agency, notes that 'some photographers already have their own archive which they then give to us to manage, but many simply don't have the time to do both' [taking and managing pictures].

The media are increasingly publishing amateur photographs sent in by readers and listeners. Although the quality is often poor, particularly when taken with camera phones, it enables hard-to-reach news or celebrity stories to be illustrated. Picture desk staff may even browse websites like Flickr, Picasa and Photobucket for relevant photographs. The more sophisticated website Scoopt offers 40% of royalties to the photographer if their image is used.

Outsourcing

Another method commercial picture archives use to reduce costs is outsourcing. Many libraries cannot afford continuously to modernize with each new technological development and do not have the resources to promote their collection. A typical scenario would see an archive digitized, stored, catalogued, captioned and transmitted by an outside contractor to whom the library subsequently pays a yearly fee to manage their sales. The contractor would ideally have an existing client base in the same area as the archive's customers. Others prefer to manage their collection in-house. Martin Atkin, Head of Creative Development at the Greenpeace Archive, says: 'We have a large internal demand for the library and it would be complicated if it was somewhere else. There is talk about making it more commercially viable in the future but just now it serves our internal needs just fine and acts as an efficient campaigning tool.'

Building your picture library career

The best picture librarians are passionate about the material with which they work. Picture archiving can be hard in the news and media industry. Shouted at by journalists, and constantly supplied with new images to process to tight deadlines, picture librarians working for newspapers, magazines and broadcasters can feel they are working in the middle of a hurricane. In reality, they are providing content for a publication or programme which will be replaced by another edition or episode in a matter of months, weeks or even days. The author remembers being surrounded by a labyrinth of the best fashion and portrait photography in the world when working for magazine publisher Condé Nast, but never having a chance to look at it because of the volume of work.

Joining the picture library industry requires the same proactive approach as other desirable sectors. Michael Martin, adviser from the Qualifications and Professional Development department of UK professional association CILIP, offers the following advice to would-be picture librarians:

> Look at how you can build up experience in your current post: it may not be in your job title or description but by getting involved in cataloguing images or promoting different materials (ideally supporting the aims and objectives in your job) you will be in a strong position to apply when that ideal post is advertised. Join the Multimedia Information Technology special interest group of CILIP; attend their conferences and short courses. Not only will this support your knowledge and C.V. but [it] will help you make good contacts and maintain your current awareness. Students are in a strong position to direct their careers. Focus on the elements of the course that really interest you. Choose, or if necessary search for, placements in media libraries. Placements may not be appropriate but you may also slant your dissertation

to the area you want to work in. This gives you material for your C.V. and examples to refer to in interviews. When you graduate that ideal job may not be advertised. Don't wait around for it to appear, build your experience and think how what you're doing can be transferred to media librarianship.

When approaching employers, a covering letter and CV is far more formal and professional than an e-mail with an attachment but should be followed up by a telephone call a week later. This demonstrates enthusiasm, initiative and courage, all useful qualities in a picture librarian.

Small professional groups like BAPLA, AUKML (Association of UK Media Librarians) or ARLIS, the art libraries' society, have paltry membership costs for students yet provide a wealth of information and events. The author attended both the AUKML and ARLIS conferences as a volunteer, after contacting the membership secretary to see if they needed an extra pair of hands, and made valuable contacts. It is advisable regularly to check relevant websites for details of social events and talks for the training and networking opportunities they provide. BAPLA offers various factsheets and training for members and non-members as well as running a free vacancy service, allowing members to gain job experience and apply for full-time positions.

Dr Paul Burton, Senior Lecturer in Computer and Information Sciences at the University of Strathclyde, offers his advice:

> Keep an eye on careers web sites such as www.jobs.ac.uk or prospects.ac.uk, and never forget that your university or college careers service is not just for the time when you are a student: it can continue to help you after graduation. Also, look carefully at advertisements for posts in picture libraries in order to identify the skills asked for and to match them to your own.

Burton adds that a degree in library studies or information science could help towards securing a position within a media library setting: 'Certainly, many of the skills and concepts taught . . . are directly applicable to media librarianship, especially in the digital age when picture libraries are creating web sites and digital versions of their collections. This is because the structure of these courses emphasize the techniques of information organization, storage and retrieval regardless of format.'

The future of picture libraries

The author's main prediction for the future of picture libraries is that there will be increasing conglomeration and digitization. In a few years the industry will be 100% online with just a few global players. The average consumer with a personal computer will soon have access to the world's collections of digital images from their desktop. Everything held in a physical space will sooner or later be digitized and hard copy used for reference or auctioned off. The structure and tools that facilitate browsing, querying and retrieval are still in their infancy, but the trend is irreversible.

Traditional photo libraries may find it hard to adapt or survive in such a changing market, particularly as further corporatization of the industry occurs. Stills collections are already being snapped up by media organizations eager not to be left behind. Large conglomerates acquire small picture libraries because they see this as an opportunity to bring together the best brands, the best collections and the best distribution into their existing sales infrastructure. To compete with the bigger picture libraries, who can do quantity deals with publishers, smaller picture libraries will need to concentrate on their marketing.

It is true that no computer in the world can replace or compete with the years of knowledge gained through being an expert in a given field. But staff roles and responsibilities must adapt and diversify to work within the digital environment and be prepared to break down the walls between individual collections. The author has worked with colleagues who cling to familiar territory, unable or unwilling to adapt to image digitization. Picture librarians are becoming the gateways to material rather than the owners. They must manage images wherever they are collected, transmitted and used.

A further challenge for expert picture archivists is to retain the development of the collection which short-sighted managers may feel is now the responsibility of the IT department (few would consider hard copy pictures to be the responsibility of facilities management, although the IT software or hardware holding the images is simply an electronic storage medium). Libraries need to work to prevent images being managed by people who are not trained in archival and preservation practices. Archivists need to consider how their uniquely well developed training and skills in handling image materials can be applied to digital images. Can librarians be expected to become digital asset managers or technologists?

The traditional customer base for images is also changing. The picture library business has become a central PR resource. Corporate websites need far better and more original images than were ever needed for their published annual report; digital outdoor media campaigns now appear everywhere from bus shelters to sports arenas; and news organizations frequently buy editorial photography rather than sending photographers out on assignment. To these new customers, picture libraries are not valued for the size of the collection and the number of transactions, but for where and how resources are accessible. Where information professionals know the great value of curated print, they place higher value on convenience and speed. The new generation of customers wants a seamless presentation of collections and services regardless of where it is held, by whom and in what format. These clients do not care about standards, or on what camera an image is taken or even how it is delivered. They simply want to be able to buy the product and use it as they wish. To conclude, Linda Royles from BAPLA outlines the essential qualities of the modern picture library:

> In the current fast moving digital landscape, talking, learning and sharing is essential in making any prediction for the rapid pace of change that is today's content environment. Associations such as BAPLA are essential for bringing together competitors, to work on best practice and to share expertise with the wider community. Dialogue between buyer and seller is essential and easier to facilitate on an industry wide basis than on a company by company offering.

Note and acknowledgements

The author's opinions do not necessarily reflect those of his employer. All quotations are derived from personal communications with the author.

Useful sources and contacts in the UK

Arts and Humanities Data Service for the Visual Arts
    (AHDS Visual Arts)
University College for the Creative Arts
Falkner Road
Farnham
Hampshire GU9 7DS
Tel: +44 (0) 1252 892 723

Fax: +44(0) 1252 892 913
E-mail: info@visualarts.ahds.ac.uk
Website: http://ahds.ac.uk/visualarts/index.htm

Associated Press (AP)
The Interchange
Oval Road
Camden Lock
London NW1 7DZ
Tel: +44 (0) 20 7482 7482
Fax: +44 (0) 20 7413 8327
Website: www.aparchive.com

British Association of Picture Libraries & Agencies (BAPLA)
18 Vine Hill
London EC1R 5DZ
Tel: +44 (0) 20 7713 5397
Fax: +44 (0) 20 7713 1211
Website: www.bapla.org.uk

Chartered Institute of Library and Information Professionals (CILIP)
7 Ridgmount Street
London WC1E 7AE
Tel: +44 (0) 20 7255 0500
Fax: +44 (0) 20 7255 0501
Textphone: +44 (0) 20 7255 0505
E-mail: info@cilip.org.uk
Website: www.cilip.org.uk

Department of Computer and Information Sciences (CIS)
The University of Strathclyde
Livingstone Tower
26 Richmond Street
Glasgow G1 1XH
Tel: +44 (0) 141 548 2934 / 3700
Fax: +44 (0) 141 548 4523
E-mail: enquiries@cis.strath.ac.uk
Website: www.strath.ac.uk/cis

Picture Research Association (PRA)
(Business hours 9 am to 5 pm UK time Monday to Friday)
c/o 1 Willow Court, off Willow St
London EC2A 4QB
Website: www.picture-research.org.uk

Pidgeon Digital
Microworld House
PO Box 35488
London NW8 6WD
Tel: +44 (0) 20 7586 4499
Fax: +44 (0) 20 7722 1068
E-mail: microworld@ndirect.co.uk
Website: www.pidgeondigital.com

Popperfoto
(Dates back to as early as 1850 with colour images from 1936. Popperfoto
claims the archive is now so irreplaceable that it ranks with museum
collections)
The Old Mill
Overstone Farm
Overstone
Northampton NN6 0AB
Tel: +44 (0) 1604 670670
Fax: +44 (0) 1604 670635
E-mail: inquiries@popperfoto.com
Website: www.popperfoto.com

Scoopt Ltd
Hillington Park
Innovation Centre
1 Ainslie Road
Glasgow G52 4RU
Tel: +44 (0) 845 888 7627
E-mail: contact@scoopt.com
Website: www.scoopt.com

Victoria and Albert Museum (V&A)
(Contains one of the oldest photographic libraries in the world)
V&A South Kensington
Cromwell Road
London SW7 2RL
Tel. +44 (0) 20 7942 2000
Website: www.vam.ac.uk

References

BAPLA (2007) *BAPLA Summer 2007 Newsletter.*
Nelsson, R. (2006) Credible and Credited: the rise of the media librarians, *Library + Information Update*, 5 (12), 41.
Taylor, C. (2007) Metadata's Many Meanings and Uses, *Ideography Briefing Paper*, www.ideography.co.uk/briefings/pdf/PB_metadata.pdf.

Chapter 4

Cataloguing television programmes

HAZEL SIMPSON
With an afterword by Katharine Schopflin

Television and radio programmes are catalogued for two reasons. First, a broadcasting organization or authority may wish to keep a record of the title, date and time a programme was transmitted. Second, anyone wanting to reuse transmitted or recorded material needs to be able to find it. For most of the history of television cataloguing, the cataloguing record has also stood as a surrogate for the programme itself, so that researchers know as much as possible about the footage they are seeking before they enter the time-consuming, and often costly, process of ordering and viewing a tape or can of film. Some television companies now archive their output as server files which can be viewed online by researchers. They are a tiny, but growing, percentage of the world's holdings of television output. However, for a researcher to locate the right bit of footage (an anachronistic term that will be used in this chapter about all moving images, no matter what format they are held in), this real media still needs to be described in words, meaning that cataloguing records are still necessary.

The bulk of this chapter will examine how the BBC (British Broadcasting Corporation, the UK's national broadcaster) catalogues its holdings of television output, one of the largest collections in existence belonging to a working broadcaster. The author, who has worked for BBC Information & Archives since 1988, primarily in its Television Archive, will examine the problems encountered and compromises made in attempting to make hundreds of thousands of hours of broadcast footage searchable and findable. In an afterword, the editor will contrast her experiences cataloguing using an online media asset

*management system for an independent news producer, and the changes which
ensued to their cataloguing technique after its introduction. Finally, she will
mention the latest developments in automated cataloguing.*

Introduction

The BBC's television cataloguing department is a small unit, part of the much
larger Information & Archives (I&A) area covering many different research
and archive holdings and services. It consists of a team of cataloguers
providing a record of television output readily accessible to researchers by
name, reporter, genre and subject. Members of the team catalogue using
an online system called INFAX. They catalogue all programmes broadcast
on the various BBC channels either by viewing them or by referring to
production paperwork. The record they produce includes basic title and
credit information, a description of the content and subject classification.
Researchers can search the catalogue by directly accessing these references
or by conducting a free text search across the shotlisting description and
classification.

INFAX and the cataloguing system

From the 1960s the BBC Film Library (as it was called then) catalogued
using a subject card index. They did not catalogue the entire output of BBC
television but described in detail any film content with high reuse value.
During this time, cataloguers were unable to view output stored on
videotape through a lack of facilities (meaning, for example, that a magazine
programme containing both film and videotape items would only have the
elements on film catalogued). A separate department, Programme Index,
kept a record of programme titles, presenters and contributors but did not
produce any subject cataloguing.

In 1984 an online catalogue was introduced. INFAX, as it came to be called
(and will be referred to throughout this chapter), began as a videotape stock
control system called VTOL. Over the years other elements, including a
film stock control system, cataloguing descriptions and subject indexing, were
added. Researchers could only access INFAX via a dumb terminal and each
user required a separate login. However, it seamlessly integrated all the
separate elements relating to the stock control and content descriptions of
television programmes. Since then, other catalogues and stock control
systems from Information and Archives' holdings have been added. Although

a system developed in the early 1980s is ancient in computer database terms, it is so integral to so many activities in the BBC that it has been difficult to replace.

Like most online systems of its time, INFAX was designed as a command-driven system for the use of highly trained experts. It is not user-friendly and cannot be used intuitively. Indeed, it looks little different today from when the author first started at the BBC in 1988. Features which would be unimaginable to database designers starting from scratch today include the lack of any 'undo' function (meaning that the accidental deletion of text is a major incident), an inability to scroll back through records when browsing a list of references or titles, clumsy word wrapping (so text disappears off screen forever if new words are inserted into a record after saving) and the limitation of characters in any text field (which has resulted in cataloguers using now-obscure abbreviations and truncations to fit text into the field). However, some improvements have been made. INFAX now runs on a terminal emulator within a Windows environment, so users can open it up and use it from their desktop. The biggest boon to users has been the introduction of a cut and paste facility, saving the need laboriously to write down complex classification numbers and retype them when searching.

What's in INFAX?

Until the 1990s the BBC broadcast on two analogue television channels: BBC One and Two. When digital transmission technology became more widespread, they were allocated more channels using digital bandwidth. At the time of writing, there are four licence-fee-funded digital channels in addition to the two original terrestrial ones: BBC Three, BBC Four, CBBC and CBeebies. Over the years the numbers of broadcasting hours on each channel has also increased. This has led to a massive increase in the volume of programmes that require cataloguing.

The BBC Television Archive does not catalogue everything broadcast. Natural history programmes are looked after by a specialist department at the Natural History Unit in Bristol; purchased programmes such as films and overseas television series are not the BBC's responsibility (although programmes commissioned by the BBC from independent companies are treated in the same way as programmes produced in-house); sports programmes have their own library; and regional programmes, apart from those made in London, are catalogued in local BBC libraries. However, in addition to programme output, the Television Archive catalogues the main daily news bulletins and stockshots drawn from untransmitted material.

BBC Television Archive's cataloguing policy is in fact now far less selective than in the past, when librarians only catalogued heavyweight programmes such as arts and science documentaries (for example, *Arena* or *Horizon*) and current affairs (*Panorama* or *Newsnight*). These types of programmes were subject-catalogued because they were considered more valuable in terms of research and reuse than other genres such as drama, light entertainment and comedy. Although it remains the case that programmes considered to have a high proportion of original and reusable content are given the most attention, programme-makers' tastes have changed. An increasing quantity of archive programmes (so-called 'clip shows') reuse comedy, popular drama and light entertainment and some of these (for example, *Pride and Prejudice* (1995), *Fawlty Towers*, *Blake's 7* and *Dinnerladies*) are now catalogued in more depth. The perceived value of a programme will govern whether it is viewed by the cataloguer, who then creates a complete shotlist, or whether they rely on paperwork produced by programme-makers, a process known as annotation level cataloguing.

Each television programme catalogued on INFAX is associated with an entry in an index of transmission called TILIST. This is an alphabetical list of (nearly) all programmes broadcast by the BBC since television resumed in 1945 after World War 2 (the BBC had previously offered a regular television broadcasting service between 1936 and 1939). In fact, TILIST is incomplete until the 1980s as until then it did not include programmes for which no recorded copy exists or to which the BBC no longer had rights of transmission. Researchers therefore will find no record of programmes before 1984 which were transmitted live or for which the film or videotape was wiped (something which was not uncommon for light entertainment or commercial music programmes considered to be of little future value, as videotape was expensive and reusable). After INFAX was introduced in 1984 all transmissions were included in TILIST.

The cataloguing process
Viewed cataloguing

Under the current system, cataloguers carry out viewed cataloguing work from a VHS cassette and shotlist the content from start to finish, noting timecodes (the VCR counter being set to zero at the start of the programme). It is a time-consuming process due to the need to stop and start the tape and write down shot descriptions. Cataloguers then return to their desks and identify which categories the different shots belong in. Different categories include independent actuality (useful BBC-copyright moving pictures that do not include identifiable individuals), dependent actuality (where a named person is identifiable), interviews, library pictures and non-BBC copyright footage. They then assign the different shots to the appropriate categories and transcribe the rearranged shotlist onto INFAX. Indexing entries are then added.

Annotation level cataloguing

In annotation level cataloguing, cataloguers do not view the programme, but use other sources of information as their basis, mainly production paperwork. The main source used is the so-called PasC or Programme as Completed form. This is a form which production staff are supposed to fill in with production details and records of the sources of all the footage used in the programme. However, PasCs do not arrive in the library for every programme. Additional sources used to complete the entry include BBC Magazines' television guide the *Radio Times*, press releases and, increasingly, the relevant web page on the BBC website, www.bbc.co.uk. When they are provided, cataloguers need to analyse PasCs for relevant information, as they contain a range of information for different purposes. If the PasC is unclear on any point, the programme may be viewed for clarity. Magazine programmes (programmes consisting of a series of small packages or interviews on different topics) such as *The Daily Politics* and *Working Lunch* benefit from this approach.

Indexing

In addition to describing the content of BBC programmes, Television Archive cataloguers also assign classification references so that they can be retrieved by subject and personality. There are two levels of subject classification. The first level is that of the 'programme idea', which aims to encapsulate the subject of the entire programme. The second level covers individual elements within the programme that might be useful in the future, such as secondary subjects and themes and, in the case of viewed programmes, individual shots and sequences.

The classification system used by BBC Television Archive cataloguers is called LONCLASS. It is an adaptation of the Universal Decimal Classification (UDC) scheme. LONCLASS stands for London Classification because it was developed for use by the main BBC film and videotape libraries which are based in London. The scheme was used for the original card catalogue and was transferred to INFAX in 1984. Even at that time it contained a great many classification numbers and it has grown since then. The large amount of class numbers and the even larger number of combinations of numbers that exist lead to quality control problems.

UDC was chosen as the basis of the TV subject catalogue classification because it is a faceted scheme. A faceted scheme allows different concepts to be linked together to provide a highly accurate description of a subject, something that is particularly useful when cataloguing television programmes which could be about literally anything. LONCLASS includes both general concepts such as GRAMMAR (for example, a schools programme on the grammar of the English language) and highly specific subjects such as JEREMY PAXMAN'S AGGRESSIVE INTERVIEW OF MICHAEL HOWARD (which was a specific moment in a broadcast from the current affairs programme *Newsnight*). Subject terms are linked together (or 'strung') using facet indicators, that is, punctuation which separates the different facets representing the subject and which indicate the type of facet (for example a number in brackets indicates the location the incident described took place). They allow precision and mean that researchers should be able to find specific things without having to wade through irrelevant material. Cataloguers place the different facets according to what is known in classification theory as citation order. This indicates the relevance of the different facets of the classification number to the topic and helps with the recall and precision of searches. Where LONCLASS differs from UDC is in the unique use of auxiliaries which advance it beyond a general subject catalogue to one aimed at singular aspects of television. For example, there are auxiliaries to describe camera movement (such as BIG CLOSE UPS) and movement within the footage (such as TAKE OFF to describe the movement of an aeroplane).

Although this sounds highly specialized (and the work of classification certainly is highly skilled), its purpose is simply to make sure that similar material is filed under the same classification number. Researchers do not need to know the classification number to find a topic, but can interrogate the system using natural language. Their results should be very precise, however, as although a concept will be identified by a single classification number, it will be associated with many different synonyms and subject terms. This is LONCLASS's great strength and enables subjects which have come to be described in very different ways or have changed their names to be filed together. This is essential in a catalogue which covers decades of something as ephemeral and finely attuned to popular culture as television programming. For example, the term HEATHROW AIRPORT files under the same classification number as LONDON AIRPORT, although it is unlikely to be referred to by this name in a television programme or its cataloguing description. Countries like ZIMBABWE (formerly known as RHODESIA) or organizations like ROYAL MAIL (which at one point was known as CONSIGNIA) also have the same classification number but can be retrieved by either term. Problems caused by synonyms are also avoided as, for example, a single classification number is used for the terms DIRECT MAILING and JUNK MAIL (and for LORRIES and TRUCKS). The researcher will bring up all the entries associated with the topic regardless of which term they used to search by.

Complicated topics can produce unwieldy subject terms, made up of individual concept descriptions separated by slashes. To avoid this problem, cataloguers create new headings attached to the complex numbers. For example, researchers looking for references about the ongoing ethnic tension in Kosovo could find them all filed under the heading KOSOVO SITUATION rather than the string VIOLENCE/RACISM/ALBANIANS/SERBS/KOSOVO. They will find the same references under the terms RACIAL CONFLICT BETWEEN SERBS AND ALBANIANS IN KOSOVO or KOSOVO RACIAL CONFLICT BETWEEN SERBS AND ALBANIANS. Classification numbers such as this one, which cover long-term ongoing stories, are also known as 'cover numbers' and are added to all stories or items related to them. Another example might be a news story about a car bomb in Baghdad, which in addition to classification numbers indicating car bombing will also have the cover number POST WAR SITUATION IN IRAQ 2003, as would the death of British soldiers in Basra. This means, for example, that somebody producing a documentary on the topic in 20 years' time should be able to retrieve all references.

The powerful search possibilities offered by stringing (combining smaller numbers which represent different facets) is diluted by a number of problems. The volume of search terms in the scheme can often feel overwhelming. Classifiers are not always consistent when they combine numbers or reverse the facets in their indexing. Some do not follow the classification rules. And problem classification numbers, known as SIQ numbers, also appear. SIQ numbers are classification numbers marked in the scheme with this code to indicate that they are duplicates, over-extended or just plain wrong.

Duplication, where two numbers representing the same subject appear, is not a common problem and duplicates are usually removed whenever possible or one number chosen over the other. Over-extended numbers, where too many irrelevant terms are added to a single number, are perhaps the most exasperating problem. The number for WOMEN is the same as the number for GIRLS and the same applies to MEN and BOYS. So a researcher looking for footage of girls playing football would have to wade through many items showing women playing football. GREEN BELTS and PARKS is another frustrating example among many more. Some numbers are simply wrong. The number attached to the term for HOUSES OF PARLIAMENT is marked as a SIQ number because it consists of the number for parliament buildings, 725.11, followed by the number for the location Westminster (421.221) and an incorrect name extension, which means it often doesn't translate correctly into natural language. Thus, the number appears as 725.11 (421.221 HOUSES OF PARLIAMENT), whereas it should be 725.11(421.221) HOUSES OF PARLIAMENT. The term ILLEGAL COAL MINING, at 343.7:622.33, has been given a classification number which puts it in the wrong place in the subject schedule, so if someone is browsing by classification number rather than searching using natural language the classification numbers preceding it and succeeding it are not relevant. In this case, the classification number for CRIMES AGAINST PROPERTY, 343.7, has been used to make up the number, so it files near crimes such as mugging and burglary and translates into natural language as OFFENCES (AGAINST PROPERTY)/COAL MINES.

When people appear in or are referred to in a programme they are normally given name references, rather than classification numbers. A huge authority file of contributors is kept up to date and efforts are made to ensure that references to the same person are kept under the same name. It is a challenge for the cataloguer to identify that an expert with a very common name appearing in an interview, say, representing Oxfam was the same man who five years earlier was described in the authority file as 'Smith, Andrew (Amnesty International)' (this example is fictitious). In exceptional circumstances, certain people are also identified by classification numbers, meaning they can be retrieved not only by their name reference, but also by subject classification. For example, a documentary on the Queen will have references for her name and the classification number for QUEEN ELIZABETH I (ROYALTY). With this example, as the Queen is someone who appears so often in television programmes, any interesting footage of her carrying out specific actions would also be classified. For example, if there were moving pictures of the Queen on horseback, the classification number would be added represented by the term BRITISH ROYAL FAMILY_ELIZABETH I QUEEN ELIZABETH II (ROYALTY):HORSE RIDING.

As with any procedure carried out over a number of years by large teams of workers, cataloguing in the BBC Television Archive is not always consistent. Individual cataloguers may tackle different programmes in the same television series with different approaches, laying out the cataloguing entry in a different way, producing differing amounts of detail, more or less indexing and even describing the overall programme in a different way, although consistency is encouraged by the creation of templates for regular television series. Some programmes in a series may not deserve as much detail as another: one week's episode of the current affairs programme *Panorama* may be full of archive or reusable independent actuality, while the next broadcast may be full of interviews, so the same detail would not be required. Although consistency is important to help guide researchers through the process of finding what they need, the advantage of having a range of approaches to cataloguing is that it may reflect different researchers' understanding of the catalogue. It is impossible accurately to predict how every researcher now and many years into the future may choose to search or understand a cataloguing entry and the one cataloguer who adds a particular index term may help a researcher locate a programme or some footage they otherwise would not have found.

INFAX's users

The BBC Television Archive catalogue can be accessed in a variety of ways by anyone (although as of July 2007 the publicly accessible web catalogue is still incomplete and being trialled). Until recently, the catalogue was only available to BBC staff either by terminal-based access to INFAX (the native, 'blue-screen', version of the database) or via its web-based version found on the BBC's intranet site. The terminal-based INFAX requires a login and password to use it and entries can only be edited in this version. Staff throughout I&A are allowed access to the native version with varying degrees of permissions. Staff in the rest of the BBC tend only to use the web-based version. With this they can access cataloguing information for television programmes (and the other archives which use the database) but not information about holdings or the classification schedule.

What used to be a closed catalogue is now an open one. What used only to be available to librarians in the enquiries department, who fielded telephone calls and ordered up VHS cassettes for customers, is now available to all. Consequently, problems relating to abbreviations, consistency and specialist terms have been exposed to the non-expert researcher. All catalogues use specialist terms unique to the content of the catalogue and INFAX is no exception. Cataloguing descriptions include common terminology used in shot description such as 'ls' for long shot or 'mcs' for medium close shot, which stand a reasonable chance of being understood by broadcasting professionals, although not by members of the public. INFAX also contains exclusive terminology such as 'acty' for actuality and 'sp s' for specially shot. Another factor which has been discovered since the catalogue was opened up is the presence of what we now see as old-fashioned language. For example, cataloguing entries from before the 1980s will describe both female children and young adult women as a 'girl'. Researchers can only tell from the context which of the two is actually depicted. What is now seen as offensive language may also appear and contemporary researchers are unlikely to carry out a free text search using problem words such as 'coloured', 'spastic' or 'dumb' (although the classification number will also be associated with what are, in current language, more acceptable terms).

Moreover, in order to cram as much information as possible into character-limited fields, cataloguers accidentally developed a new language many years before the emergence of text speak. Abbreviations like 'ppl' for people, 'w' for with, 'abt' for about and 'hosp' for hospital are self-explanatory, but some abbreviations may have seemed clear to the cataloguer when they originally used them but have become less so with time. Even when the meaning of these abbreviations is clear in the context of the cataloguing entry, they are often ugly and break up the flow of the text. More importantly researchers will not find them using a free text search: no one is likely to look for 'Hammersmith Hosp' rather than 'Hammersmith Hospital'.

This was something which mattered less when all the searching on the catalogue was done by qualified librarians who had once been cataloguers themselves, as they knew to search under the classification term for HAMMERSMITH HOSPITAL rather than in the free text. But now that INFAX is searchable on the web by end-users who mostly only know how to carry out free text searches, there is the danger that searchers are missing out on important entries because their searches are producing false negative results (and it is a feature of research that people do not know to look for what they do not know exists). Free text searches are, moreover, likely to produce a high recall in results (it was precisely to avoid this that such a complex classification system was developed in the first place) meaning that the researcher will either need painstakingly to browse through pages of results or will simply choose the first results that appear and possibly miss out on the most relevant footage for their programme. It is not possible to go back over all the catalogue entries (there are literally hundreds of thousands) to redo previously abbreviated descriptions but, since the introduction of the web browser made the catalogue available to non-expert researchers, the use of abbreviations has been strongly discouraged among cataloguers.

The future

At time of writing, LONCLASS has been in use for 40 or more years and INFAX in its current form for nearly 15, which is a testament to its robustness. Future developments include the proposed introduction of computer-assisted indexing using the LONCLASS classification scheme. It is hoped that this will speed up the process of indexing and enable an ever-increasing quantity of broadcast output to be retrievable. Such software needs careful training and correction, however. There are no plans to replace all cataloguers with an automated system at present.

Afterword: cataloguing using a media asset management system at ITN
by Katharine Schopflin

ITN (Independent Television News) is an independent news provider making news bulletins for commercial British terrestrial television channels. It additionally runs a busy archive sales business, ITN Source, which introduced a digital asset management (DAM) system into the business in July 2006 for the use of cataloguers and researchers. From this time, cataloguing entries included not just shot descriptions, time codes and tape numbers, but quick-time versions of the actual footage to which they referred. Footage that ITN has the rights to sell also publishes onto the open web on the website www.itnsource.com and can be purchased using an e-commerce system (although the majority of sales still take place using ITN Source's sales team). The introduction of the system has changed the emphasis in the cataloguing of new material from describing individual shots in detail, to summarizing the pictures using well-chosen words and ensuring only appropriate material will be published to the ITN website.

New activities carried out by archive staff using the DAM system include republishing archived clips onto a dedicated server under agreed naming conventions and attaching these clips to cataloguing shotlists. There are also changes associated with material being published on the world wide web. Clearly, ITN can only publish material on the open web which it has the rights to sell. Copyright sourcing had always been part of ITN shotlists, but now the assignment of copyrights to individual pieces of footage is a vital part of separating material that ITN Source can sell, and which can therefore publish onto the website, from those which cannot. Shotlisters now have the responsibility to divide specific frames (there are 24 frames per second of moving pictures) from those which will publish and those which will not.

As footage now has a publicly accessible life much longer than the original broadcast, cataloguers also now need to assign restrictions on saleable pictures to prevent the publication of material which may have been licensed for a single broadcast (such as commercial music) or agreed for an individual programme (such as the appearance of minors). Other restrictions might be added onto material which was not broadcast on UK television, as it comes from one of the archives ITN Source has been commissioned to manage by a third party. Output from these 'partner archives' (most notably the news wire service Reuters) may include footage not acceptable to UK viewers on taste and decency grounds and a restriction might therefore be added to prevent it being published on the web. Because the pictures on the web can be accessed by anyone in the world with internet access, one highly important area of restriction concerns anonymity risks, where an individual facing civil liberty restrictions in a foreign territory might be comfortable with being filmed for broadcast in the UK, but whose life might be endangered if the same footage were seen in their own country.

There are now four categories of researcher searching the ITN catalogue: a small number of expert archive researchers working for ITN newsrooms; news staff, normally journalists, who are expected to carry out most of their own archive research; ITN Source sales staff, responding to queries from external clients wishing to buy footage; and members of the public. Researchers in the first three categories access the catalogue on the ITN intranet and have access to all footage that is archived, regardless of copyright and restrictions (although copyright and restriction information is made very clear in the cataloguing entry and it is their responsibility to make sure they use the footage responsibly). Members of the public can access all the catalogue entries (except in a few cases where restrictions will exclude cataloguing text from publication, normally for anonymity risk reasons), browse saleable footage and in some circumstances even purchase it online.

As at the BBC, increasing numbers of non-expert researchers accessing cataloguing entries has changed the way ITN shotlisters catalogue. Difficult words, abbreviations and technical jargon are kept to a minimum, or are explained in parentheses in cataloguing entries. This is important not just for those accessing the catalogue outside the industry (for example, those wishing to license material for educational purposes) but also for younger people working in broadcasting, who may lack experience or expertise. This particularly affects those working in independent production, where staff often carry out a range of tasks including production management, reporting and videotape editing as well as archive research, and may not be expert in the latter.

Unlike at the BBC, there is no subject classification in the ITN catalogue, which means that shotlisters are encouraged to include as many synonyms as possible to enable current and future entries to be retrieved. This does not, of course, help with older shotlists which may only describe the footage in the language used at the time and depend on researchers trying out different search terms in order to find the footage they are seeking. This problem may be solved in the future when it is hoped that an element of language control will be introduced, possibly by allowing the search to reference a taxonomy so that, for example, a researcher looking for early material showing nuclear power stations would find them even though the original shotlister had described them with the term 'atomic power', a term they might never think of using.

A more radical change to shotlisting style than the extension of the catalogue to new users is the fact that the cataloguing entry no longer needs to act as a surrogate for the film. This means that complex shot descriptions (which may use terms like 'close up', 'low angle view', 'tilt down', 'pan' or 'track' to describe specific camera angles or movements) are not necessary as the researcher can see what the pictures look like themselves. Moreover, whereas ITN shotlisters had previously listed every shot that appeared in a piece of footage, they can now summarize a sequence in a single sentence. For example a sequence which might previously have been catalogued like this entirely fictitious entry:

> Black car arriving at hospital carrying Tony Blair MP (Prime
> Minister) and others PAN Car stopping and Blair exiting
> Close up of Blair greeting hospital officials PULL FOCUS
> General view of hospital in background
> Blair and officials into hospital

would now be more likely simply to appear as 'Tony Blair MP (Prime Minister) arriving at hospital, greeting officials and entering'. How much extra detail is added depends on how much information can be gathered and how important the shotlister deems such information as the make of car, names of hospital officials, what Blair is wearing or which wing of the hospital is being visited. This makes the cataloguing entry far simpler to read and allows the shotlisters more time to consider which words really add value to an entry to help a researcher find the pictures they need and, potentially, to catalogue a far greater volume of material in a shorter period of time.

Automated cataloguing

Cataloguing television programmes is a time-consuming process, requiring significant numbers of expensive skilled employees. While it is accepted by many television companies that there is significant value in having their moving images retrievable for reuse or resale, they are understandably concerned to find ways of speeding up the process, especially as the quantity of output increases to fill increasing numbers of broadcast platforms. One area currently being developed is that of automated cataloguing, whereby artificial intelligence enables computer software to recognize images and describe them, so that previously unsearchable pictures are converted into text which can then be interrogated by an online search. There is increasing scientific research into this area and a number of commercial database companies offer products which claim to carry out automatic or computer-assisted cataloguing.

Information the software might look at to decide what the pictures are about includes voice-over descriptions, on-screen captions and analysis of the pixels making up the picture. The latter might enable the software to recognize that a particular arrangement of pixels was a dog, a sunset or even President George W. Bush, particularly if the software were given extensive training. However, in the editor's opinion, research is at an early stage and any software faces considerable limitations. First, any cataloguer will bring a range of knowledge, research and external information sources to their analysis of moving images, of which voice-over narration and captions are only two. Second, these latter very rarely describe the pictures, as they are seen by broadcasters as providing information which is not immediately apparent in the pictures (this has also been a limitation in the automated cataloguing of still images, whose captions rarely describe what is in the picture). Third, in cataloguing, context is all. The fact that software can recognize that a set of pixels is President Bush may not help establish that, in a specific sequence, he is visiting a US airbase on a day in which his party has had a poor showing in the opinion polls. Similarly, even if (as is not yet the case in any of the commercial products) the software could identify that a dog was a pit bull terrier, it could not suggest whether this was a banned breed of dog in the country in which it is depicted.

As has been seen in this chapter, the challenge for television cataloguers is to make moving images findable by describing them using words. One of the great advantages of words is that, in addition to being searchable in free text, clusters of words can be associated with specific concepts, and automated cataloguing products also often include automated classification (or computer-assisted indexing) software. This kind of software, which can be seen in commercial search engines such as Clusty (www.clusty.com), develops semantic relationships between words so that, for example, the word 'pit bull' would be associated with the word 'dog' (and may even identify one concept as a subcategory of the other). It may or may not reference an existing taxonomy, in which an information professional has already made the associations between the terms. However, although useful in many ways, this software also remains at an early stage of development and remains, in the editor's opinion, something of a blunt instrument although perhaps useful as a preliminary sorter before proper classification is carried out by librarians.

Finally, as this chapter demonstrates, the range of complex issues facing television cataloguers is constantly changing and as human beings cataloguers can respond to those changes. Most offer excellent value for money in identifying the importance of what they see and describing it accordingly, not only for expert or contemporary researchers, but for anyone searching the catalogue long into the future. The development of media asset management systems means that the value of assigning copyright sourcing and judging the appropriateness of an image to be published is greater than ever. It may be that, as automated cataloguing software becomes cheaper, it will be more economical than a person in describing and classifying large quantities of moving images, particularly if they are of a routine and repetitive nature (for example, footage of parliamentary or courtroom sessions). At present, the value added by intelligent television cataloguing would be hard to surpass in an automated product.

Chapter 5

The virtual media library (II): managing online subscriptions

JOANNE PLAYFOOT and
KATHARINE SCHOPFLIN

Most modern media libraries are as much, if not exclusively, virtual spaces as physical ones. Holding reference information in online databases rather than books on shelves has given many managers the idea that the library can be dispensed with. Yet authoritative subscription products do not appear on the company intranet or desktop by accident. Considerable work has been put in by those managing the subscriptions, to ensure that the right product has been selected, at the right price, on the right platform in such a way that their users can access it transparently and know how to use it. They may also have given time to send regular feedback to the online publishers or attend focus groups to ensure that the product remains useful and relevant. Many of these issues were faced by librarians managing reference subscriptions in hard copy. However, new issues have emerged which are specific to products being online, issues which media librarians, normally the earliest users in their organizations of online products like Dialog, DataStar and FT Profile, are ideally placed to confront.

The authors have extensive experience administering and managing online subscriptions. Joanne Playfoot manages the InfoCentre information team at IPC Magazines, publisher of consumer and lifestyle titles. Managing and controlling users' access to subscription products within the library has given their unit new status and prominence within the organization. Katharine Schopflin has worked with online subscriptions for a number of employers, most notably for BBC Information & Archives' research.gateway intranet site, where she acted as the liaison point between vendors and users. They bring their experience to examine some of the main issues that emerge when managing online subscriptions and why it is important this is done by information staff. A media library's news database subscription is likely to be at the centre of its subscription portfolio, and this chapter looks at this kind of subscription specifically first. However, many media libraries also subscribe to online products offering future events information, biographies or material concerning subject specialisms such as finance, celebrities or defence and the chapter also looks at more general subscription management issues.

History

In a talk given in 2004, Ian Watson neatly summed up the gradual opening up of online access from the specialists to the end-user:

> Until the early 1990s the internet was a world inhabited by scientists who had access to expensive mainframe computers. In the 1970s online information hosts such as *Dialog* and *DataStar* began the creation of a quite separate electronic information world, this one inhabited mostly by librarians and information specialists who acted as intermediaries. The arrival of the World Wide Web in the early 1990s forced these two worlds into collision, thrusting online information into the mainstream of popular culture and changing for ever the nature of the information business.

When Joanne Playfoot began working in the InfoCentre at IPC Media in 1999, they were one of the only departments with internet access, so it made sense for them to be in control of the company's access to online information. The original products to which the InfoCentre subscribed were Lexis Research, Dialog and, for a short period, the Companies House database. They also subscribed to hard copy versions of *Spotlight*, *Foresight News*, *Entertainment News* and *Red Pages* among other titles, all of which they subsequently subscribed to online. At this time the majority of research using online databases was undertaken by the information team, not the journalists, although a few had individual access to LexisNexis or used it in the InfoCentre.

News databases, collections of newspaper articles disaggregated from the newspapers, were one of the great innovations of 1980s, allowing information professionals to use keyword searching with a sophisticated command language to search many publications simultaneously. At the end of the 1990s, providers began to develop web-accessible versions. By the early 2000s, it was perceived that the end-users in media organizations were using the internet and ready to do their own online searching. At the same time, the publishers of stalwart library reference works such as *Encyclopaedia Britannica* and the *Oxford English Dictionary* began to offer online versions of their products (some of which had previously been available in electronic form via CD-ROM). The numbers proliferated during the decade and products like KnowUK, XreferPlus (now called CredoReference) and Oxford Reference Online acted as virtual mini-libraries, allowing users to search many publications simultaneously. These too could be rolled out to end-users.

Their experience handling hard-copy subscriptions meant librarians had the right skills to manage and control the acquisition and usage of these products. New roles emerged specializing in the particular issues concerned with electronic products. At the same time, many managers felt the availability of online products meant librarians were themselves no longer necessary, that they were defined not by their searching and evaluating skills, but by their ownership of information products. Giving journalists access to online newspaper archives encouraged libraries to cease employing staff to classify newspaper articles by subject and personality and cut and file them. The world was to become free of hard copy and seamlessly online. As we shall see, the issues are complex, and implications far from straightforward.

News databases
Introduction

In many media organizations, the news database is the only product which is made available to all users and for all it is at the heart of their 'electronic library'. These databases are the literal online manifestation of the main function of the traditional news library cuttings 'morgue'. If a library rolls out a news database across their organization, the subscription is also likely to be far and away their most expensive product; in some cases it may even cost more than staff or accommodation.

There are currently several news database products on the market. At IPC they subscribe to LexisNexis News and Business. This replaced a previous subscription to LexisNexis Professional and gives them access to newspaper articles, company reports, industry and company information and biographies. The IPC Press Office subscribes directly to LexisNexis

Professional as they require daily news alerts, something not available on News and Business, but their subscription gives them access to news and biographies only. Until recently, the two other market leaders were Thomson Business Intelligence, which no longer markets its product Dialog, and Dow Jones' Factiva. They all have fairly comprehensive coverage of the main UK and US newspapers but have exclusive content (for example, Factiva is stronger on Australian newspapers than its rivals). New entrants into the market include Moreover and NewsBank. This chapter does not propose to analyse in detail the various products' advantages and disadvantages, but which you choose will depend on your needs as regards content, user interface, price (both actual costs and pricing model) and customer service.

In the early 1990s UK newspaper libraries, led by Associated Newspapers' Steve Torrington, set up what was known as the Fleet Street data exchange (Nelsson, 2006). The libraries were paying huge fees to access online content which, in many cases, had originated with their own organizations. The system, overseen by the relevant collecting agency, the Newspaper Licensing Agency (NLA), allowed participating libraries to exchange their own paper's news feeds for access to those of other people. Today the system includes the main national daily newspapers, so subscribers need only use their online products for other publications and more complex searches.

Customized user interfaces

The off-the-shelf product sold by their news database vendor meets all the needs of many libraries, whether it is only used in the library or is rolled out to end-users. Others feel that the 'native' product is too specialized and complex for end-user searching, although most vendors have redesigned their products in recent years with the non-expert in mind. In this case they may opt to develop a customized user interface (CUI) in which content, searching options and design are specially tailored. At IPC, the CUI was developed in 2003 as a joint project between the InfoCentre team and Lexis engineers. The idea was to reduce over-usage of the system and bring down costs so that they could maintain an affordable subscription with the provider. Media libraries vary in their approaches. At the *Guardian* end-user access is given only to the Fleet Street data exchange content. Users need to come to the library if they want a search carried out on their subscription product, Factiva. This means that the expensive subscription product is only used by expert searchers and only where sources other than the UK national daily newspapers are not sufficient.

Content

To cut costs, IPC limited the number of sources available to search, while still providing a range of national and international publications so that users could access good overall source material. On their CUI, users cannot search an 'All Publications' group. Instead, the InfoCentre selected publications to make up their own bespoke groups. Some of these, such as 'UK Tabloids' and 'UK Broadsheets', were straightforward. Others, such as 'US Major Nationals', were chosen from the publications with the biggest circulation around the country. Others were standard source groups supplied by LexisNexis themselves, such as 'Major World Newspapers'. If anyone requests a specific source that is not available on the existing screen, InfoCentre staff still have access to the off-the-shelf product and can carry out the research as an enquiry.

Search screen

It was decided that IPC journalists and editors were unlikely to spend much time on the 'Power Search' (or advanced search) screen of the database (although it was of course retained for expert searchers). Instead, the 'Easy Search' page was tweaked so that it suited IPC users' needs. InfoCentre staff undertook a number of interviews with regular and heavy users of Lexis to see what sort of methods they used to search and how they used connectors and keywords. For example, in addition to the basic possibilities offered on the off-the-shelf screen, they added some more specific and straightforward commands such as '3 or More Mentions' and 'At the Start' in the drop down boxes for the end-users. On the advanced search screen, an information professional would know the command language needed to gain this specificity (in these cases 'atl3' and 'hlead') but this approach gave journalists the opportunity to search more accurately without having to know the technical jargon. They also added an optional page for users to search specifically for biographies.

The biggest customization of the search screen was the addition of a number of preset search strings which the end-user could add to their own keywords to produce more specific results. These strings included around 20–30 pre-selected keywords chosen by the InfoCentre team. These options were added to give focus and precision to the often vague searches carried out by end-users, many of whom did not even use the preset commands in the CUI and rarely used specific enough keywords. Their recall was huge and most had neither the time, the experience nor the patience to scroll through them and would simply choose the first two examples or abandon the search. Others have found journalists are often prepared to give up hours of their time to trawl through useless results rather than speak to a librarian who produces accurate results in minutes (Dunn, 2005). In neither case was it typical end-user behaviour to return to the search screen and focus their result using more keywords or field searching.

Developing a CUI is one of the few means librarians have of controlling how their users access information in the online world. When they were the gatekeepers to information, media librarians could make sure that if incorrect or incomplete information was published or broadcast, it was not down to them. Now, we have no way of stopping journalists consulting any number of unreliable sources and using poor searching techniques. Guiding end-users through good design and limiting content is one means of controlling both what they retrieve and how much it costs. It can also raise the profile of the library among its users. At IPC, enquiries increased after the product was rolled out partly because users became aware of other products and services they offered as a result of attending training sessions (Playfoot, 2006).

However, CUI development can be both an expensive initial cost (the vendor is likely to use a third party designer and charge you for this) and cost time and money to maintain. For example, you may have agreed to have your library logo or telephone contact number as part of the interface. If either of these should change (no doubt the result of organizational developments beyond the library's control) you may well be charged to update the site, even if you pay a monthly maintenance charge for support in addition to cost of the actual content. And feeding back problems to the supplier from what may now be thousands of end-users can require a new full-time post (as happened when the BBC rolled out their CUI in 1999). Moreover, the rate of change on the web is fast. Your interface may look out of date very quickly and no longer meet the needs of users whose experience with online products will be different from when you developed it. Changing the look and feel of a site can attract complaints from loyal users but leaving it unchanged makes the library look old-fashioned and out of touch. If development money for a redesign is not present, you may find yourself buying the off-the-shelf product, which has been developed at the vendor's expense, after all.

Training

Whether they subscribe to an off-the-shelf product or use the native product, libraries have the choice of training end-users themselves (and they are likely to be the most expert users) or using a trainer supplied by the vendor. The advantage of the former is that it provides a showcase for library searching skills and lets users know that if they are unable to find something, it may not mean that it is not there. Assuming there is still an enquiry service offered, they can then go to the library for help. This also gives them more flexibility in terms of when, where and how the training takes place. As a previous chapter indicated, journalists are reluctant to attend anything called a training session and the best results come from targeted one-to-one coaching. However, training consumes large quantities of staff time and if your library is heavily involved with processing data or has a heavy enquiry load, you may find it easier to hold external training sessions. If you can, make sure these are included in your contract, as vendors often charge high fees for training. Some vendors will be happier to offer free training than others. Under a contract they held in the early 2000s, the BBC's then supplier LexisNexis offered users of the native product free sessions in economical searching.

Young journalists are increasingly used to having access to online news databases and, in a change in user behaviour from some years ago, are likely to expect one to be available when they start working for a media company. To capitalize on the already perceived value of their product, when LexisNexis was rolled out at IPC in 2003, it was advertised throughout the organization, but access was only given to staff visiting the InfoCentre first for training. New joiners still attend an hour-long training session in order to receive their passwords. Initially, IPC staff trained staff themselves but headcount freezes following staff departures made this impossible. Today LexisNexis themselves carry out the training but the sessions are specifically designed around their CUI. IPC have found that training is a good way to regulate and monitor usage and provides useful information to bring to the negotiating table when the contract is up for renewal. The InfoCentre also sends each new user an easy-to-use guide to the interface, which should help them after the initial training session. They are also entitled to contact the library with any enquiries about the best methods to use.

Subscription rates

Vendors offer various different charging models. In the days when users, mostly information professionals, used the native online product, one supplier charged users for the time they were connected plus a charge per line of text downloaded. Where this was made available to end-users who lacked searching skills, the costs were phenomenal. Other models gave users a set amount (say 20 hours) of connect time per month for a flat rate, which was more economical, but users were apt to run out of credit before the end of the month and buying more hours was twice as expensive. Most common now is a model whereby users agree a monthly rate, which is monitored by the vendors (based on document downloads). If they spend more than the agreed amount, expensive penalties ensue. Where CUIs are developed it is possible to negotiate an annual charge for unlimited usage, based on the sources included in your product, possibly including charges for technical support and development. This is an expensive option. Sometimes models are combined. At one point BBC Information & Archives were paying a flat rate for the content on their CUI, but were also paying a monthly charge for the native product which was only available to information staff.

End-users are apt to overuse news databases, even after training. Overuse is more often a feature of media organizations where there is no information department. At ITN, where the news information department was closed in 2001, newsroom staff used LexisNexis on a rate of ten times more than the agreed monthly rate. As there were no penalties under the terms of that contract, this did not matter at the time, but was an issue they had to face when the contract expired. IPC initially suffered heavily from overuse by end-users, paying penalties for usage which their own expert researchers would never have incurred. In 2004, on the insistence of their provider, their previous flat rate was changed to charge for usage. This is monitored by the InfoCentre and they have the authority to report overusage to end-users' line managers and insist that the user undertake more training. If they refuse, their access to the database is removed.

Managing other subscriptions

It is to the advantage of an organization to have subscriptions controlled centrally, rather than scattered across the company under limited-user licences. Many vendors know that they rely on good relations with their libraries, but the less scrupulous will target end-users directly, even when they already have access to the product via the library. After all, it is the library's fault if they have not promoted the product sufficiently that the end-user is aware of it. It can be a good selling point for libraries under pressure to prove their worth by showing how much money they can save the organization by selecting good products and negotiating competitive rates for their use across the whole organization. At IPC all but one or two company-wide subscriptions are now managed by the library.

Heslop and MacDonald observed (2007) that providing access to these subscriptions can reduce the number of simple queries received by the library, leaving staff time to deal with more complex requests. Most end-users are capable of querying online biographical or encyclopaedic databases. At the *Guardian*, *Who's Who* and *Encyclopaedia Britannica* sit on the home page of ResearchNet, their research intranet, and users click on a link to be taken directly to the external site. At IPC the experience has been slightly different. Although the InfoCentre receives a large number of enquiries they tend to be requests for hard-copy archive material. This is significant at IPC as they hold cuttings files taken from publications not available online (such as women's lifestyle magazines) and classified in ways not easily accessed online (for example, subject areas like 'star-crossed lovers' or 'speed dating'). They also carry out online enquiries but these tend to be quick reference requests.

Choosing your products

At IPC, where the majority of publications concentrate on celebrity, lifestyle, hobbies and 'real-life' stories, they subscribe to the following titles:

- Red Pages (Profile Group)
  This resource is requested daily. It is mainly used by journalists to find contact details for major figures for interviews and publicity.
- Foresight News (Profile Group)
  This is used on an ad-hoc basis to find out about upcoming events such as charity events, film premieres and releases, interesting public days (humorous, political, social awareness, and so on), which can then be used in forthcoming issues of all the company's magazines.

- Spotlight
  This provides contact details and credits for all actors, not necessarily well known ones (who are the only ones who would appear in Red Pages).
- Cameo
  This contains addresses taken from the electoral roll. It is heavily used by reality magazines when trying to contact people for possible follow-up stories.

What you choose in your own library will depend on what you publish or broadcast but the selection of titles is a key skill. Libraries should bring their experience of hard copy products to help them evaluate the product once it has become available online. The experience of research staff is invaluable when selecting titles as they are in the best position to anticipate journalists' needs. However, if you are subscribing to online products on the basis that you are receiving fewer research requests, or expect to be in the future, then your data may be out of date. Journalists may already be finding information elsewhere and only using the enquiry service to fill the gaps.

If you manage your online subscriptions separately from your enquiry team, you are likely to meet resistance from research staff who see the rolling out of these products as a threat to their positions. Careful diplomacy is needed as you will need their help. They are not only the most knowledge-able of end-user needs but also the most expert in the organization at online searching. Moreover, librarians' knowledge of the range of sources available means they are less gullible than end-users when it comes to selecting sources. At the BBC they once trialled a database which aggregated material on the subject of international terrorism. Users in the newsroom embraced the product, saying they simply could not afford to be without it, until information staff pointed out that most of the content on this expensive product was available either free on the web or from existing subscriptions.

When online end-user products first appeared, there were few enough of them that many libraries simply subscribed to their most-used reference books online. At the time the publisher would often provide a free hard copy as part of the deal. Today, there are so many products available that careful selection is needed, especially since your acquisitions budget is not likely to be larger and online products are far more expensive than their hard copy equivalents (at IPC their budget was cut at just the time their subscription costs increased). Ironically, as Katharine Schopflin warned in 2003, the online library can be less diverse than its hard copy equivalent. Where a library may once have had access to country information from hard copies of books from Europa Publications, *The Statesman's Yearbook*, *The Economist* and *The World Guide*, which represent radically different world-views and collect statistics independently of each other, they are likely only to be able to justify subscribing online to a single one of these titles.

Bear in mind that you do not own anything in an electronic library. Whereas you could keep your hard copy reference books for as long as you could afford to store them, your online subscription only purchases you temporary access. If you let the subscription lapse, you do not retain access to less up-to-date information. Electronic journal providers are increasingly providing models whereby users, which are mostly academic libraries, can retain access to archives even if they no longer subscribe to new issues. However, the information contained in most online reference works is not discrete and cannot be separated. There is no such thing as a 'snapshot' of the 2007 edition of *Encyclopaedia Britannica*. It changes every day.

User testing

Most online products are available for free trial periods. It is a good idea to assemble a group of tame users who can try the products out in real-life situations. Ideally these would include end-users, but in reality it is very difficult to find volunteers. At IPC magazines they found that the effort to gain any feedback from them was not worth the results and today subscriptions are tested in the InfoCentre by information staff. As people who interrogate online systems every day, most research librarians have a good idea of good and bad features of online products, if they can spare the time to help. However, you can speed up the process by devising a pro-forma.

It is also an essential part of the library's role to attend focus groups and user-testing sessions with your vendors. This will make sure that the content, design and searching experience has more of a chance of suiting your end-users. Vendors design their products to reach as wide an audience as possible. In the early 2000s, Katharine Schopflin found several times that vendors changed subscription products radically without consulting or even informing their customers, to suit other markets or territories. More is known about usability now, but it is important to be proactive in this matter and keep in touch with your providers.

Site licences

As with news databases, the library can choose whether they keep their online subscriptions within the library, or roll them out to the whole organization. If they do the latter, they are likely to purchase a number of site licences, which allow an agreed number of users to use the product simultaneously. Subscribers need to guess in advance how popular a product is likely to be. Sometimes this is impossible to tell until the library starts to receive complaints from end-users who are unable to access it because too many people are already logged in. With time, usage statistics will help to inform the decision.

Some suppliers will sell unlimited user access to media libraries based on the number of people within the organization. For popular products, and to avoid disappointing end-users, this can be well worth purchasing. However, it is worth noting that it can be expensive for media libraries which, even if they are in the public sector (that is, are national broadcasters), are charged a 'commercial' rate far higher than that charged to public and academic libraries. Moreover, large media companies may have a huge staff of which maybe only a small percentage are ever potential users of the product. Librarians should bring these aspects to the negotiating table.

Technical issues

If the library controls access to online subscriptions, they are likely to be the first point of contact for complaints if technical problems arise, even if this is due to a remote technical failure nothing to do with their organization's network. It is important to build good relations both with internal IT staff and with the technologists who develop the products for your vendor. You need to have a good understanding of the problems that might arise and learn to speak technical language, or you will not be taken seriously. It can be difficult to meet end-user expectations. End-users may be unsatisfied with well indexed subscription products, which load more slowly than search engines. Diplomacy and tact are essential when mediating between frustrated end-users and remote technical staff, neither of whom has any notion of how the situation presents to each other.

These relationships are also important when acquiring online. Although this is less of a problem than it used to be, as products are now more likely to be available on multiple platforms, you will need to know what kinds of hardware, operating systems and web browsers are used across the organization and to check that the product is compatible with all of them. You should also ask if the product you are buying is compatible with additional software such as screenreading tools for users with visual impairments. These issues make purchasing online products more than simply a matter of signing a cheque.

Passwords

Libraries that make a range of products available to end-users may find that end-users find remembering different passwords to use each one confusing and off-putting. One way of avoiding this problem is to arrange with your supplier to access their products via Internet Protocol (IP) recognition. All of the computers in your organization will have an IP address within a range of numbers and the products to which you subscribe can be set up to recognize them. Sometimes you will be given a special URL configured for IP recognition and will need to link to this page from your intranet. Some providers are unable for technical reasons or unwilling to offer IP access. It is also not possible to offer it to staff working out of the office, unless they are using a registered work laptop or PC. This is a problem as users' resistance to passwords is increasing as they have become accustomed to using tools which avoid them, for example, company-wide software, which picks up user logins to the operating system and applies them to all internal databases.

IP recognition can also be a problem as it enables staff to use products without coming through the library or having been properly trained on them. The library has more control with password access. It is important to try to ensure that users can only access products through your intranet so that it is associated with the library which, after all, has selected it, configured it and paid for it. Journalists tend not to care where their information comes from and, as Heslop and MacDonald (2007) point out, are apt to follow the link once, copy the URL and not return to the intranet again. Users are more likely to use other features of the intranet if they have to come through the site. They quote Steve Torrington at the Associated Press, who designed his intranet, E-Lib, so that users have to log in each time they want to access databases. Torrington felt that annoying some users was less important than informing all of them that they would not have the resource were it not for the library. However, if you do manage your subscriptions with passwords, make sure that they are changed frequently so that staff who leave the company are no longer able to use the databases.

Statistics

Records of how many people are using your online products and how often are essential when deciding whether or not to renew, how much you should pay or how many users licences you need. Most vendors will provide user statistics. Helen Cooke of Sage Publications (2007) is typical of a publisher who recognizes the importance of usage statistics when negotiating subscriptions, given that in many cases the library does not actually see users any more. It is worth remembering that there are a number of different approaches to gathering usage statistics, so data may not be comparable across different products. This is important as your statistics are likely to be taken very seriously by managers and finance departments. Managers at the BBC once attempted to justify the disposal of their lending book collection by comparing the number of hits received by the KnowUK site with the number of book issues, data which was in no way comparable.

Implications of the virtual library

Young journalists, editors and programme-makers arriving at media organizations expect to carry out most of their research online. Many of them will not be aware of what a media library can offer them and will assume their own searching approach is the best - indeed the only - means of research. They enjoy searching for their own information and are reluctant to give up this control to someone with better searching skills. Yet their own searching skills are often poor and consist entirely of basic freetext searching using Google and Wikipedia. Few use more than one search engine or have ever seen the advanced searching screen. If they have, they are often unsure of which field to use or worry that they would miss something if they focused their searches. They have little idea of how to evaluate sources for accuracy, reliability, currency or bias. As has been shown, they rarely know how to focus their database searches and prefer copious results from the most readily available source rather than fewer, more accurate results.

Lindsey Sellors (2007), who trains end-users at the BBC, believes that things are slowly changing and journalists are less likely to believe everything they read on the internet. Experienced journalists may even have learned to trust authoritative sources because of problems resulting from the publication of inaccurate data. However, she often encounters young journalists who feel that Wikipedia is the only site they need to use. British newspapers and broadcasters, including the BBC, were recently embarrassed after publishing obituaries of composer Ronnie Hazlehurst to whom they wrongly attributed composition of a pop song (Orlowski, 2007). Sellors points out that their own internal music database would have revealed this information with a basic search, but the users took their information from Wikipedia (and possibly only because this was the highest ranking result for the subject's name when searched in Google). This is despite the fact that in a recent exchange on the NewsLib e-mail discussion list, Wikipedia's founder Jimmy Wales (2007) wrote 'I would never recommend Wikipedia as a sole source.'

Journalists instinctively search for the 'one-stop shop'. One end-user once complained to BBC research.gateway that having to search more than one product to find out the information she needed was 'time-consuming and complicated'. However, Sellors adds that 'plugging authoritative sources is like pushing on an open door' and notes a positive development whereby a recent Broadcast Journalist position was advertised at a local radio station, which whittled 1000 applications down to 70 by rejecting all those that cited Wikipedia as their main or sole source of parliamentary information. She also feels that journalists' search skills are improving and notes far fewer complaints from end-users about too much irrelevant material being returned (which inevitably turns out to be because they tried to search using a single keyword).

At IPC they have chosen to keep certain products within the information team. This ensures that usage figures are kept under control and that the InfoCentre remains an important resource within the company. However, in many organizations, funding for electronic resources may be contingent on making them available across the organization and even on closing the library altogether. Even at IPC, it is thought that although staff numbers dwindled when there was cost-cutting across the board, the rationale for downsizing the library was the availability of online products. This underlines a central theme of online subscriptions, that they can make the library invisible and, without promotion of information staff's searching expertise, underused and expendable.

Even without their successful CUI, customers were likely to turn away from the InfoCentre because younger searchers are less familiar with the notion of information being available in a physical space. However, as mentioned before, enquiry numbers have not radically dropped. Journalists know the InfoCentre will always provide reliable information, as evidenced by the fact that they often come back to them to provide factual background for a topic they have first encountered on the web.

Resources like IPC's InfoCentre would be sorely missed if they were to disappear completely on the basis that information was 'all online'. Who would organize access to these miracle systems or deal with information providers? Without central information services to control subscriptions it is hard to know how many individual departments would have replica contracts. At ITN, where there is no information department, the news database subscription is controlled by the ITV newsroom's chief operating officer, who needed persuasion that the subscription needed renewing since it was 'all on the web'. This should act as a warning to information departments that they must ensure not only that they retain control of online subscriptions but also that the fundholders and decision-makers understand why they are important. As Ian Watson said: 'Information of all kinds is available at the click of mouse. But doctors and lawyers are not going out of business as a result of sophisticated medical and legal information sources on the web' (2004). Online subscriptions should be sourced, managed and organized by the people who know the systems the best: the information professionals.

References

Cooke, H. (2007) How Publishers are Changing the Way They Deal With Libraries, *Publishing and the Library of the Future* (conference presentation, 11 July), http://www.alpsp.org/ngen_public/article.asp?id=335&did=47&aid= 877&st=&oaid=-1.

Dunn, J. (2005) If Media Libraries Didn't Exist We Would Have to Invent Them, *Essential Skills for Information* (conference presentation, 12 March).

Heslop, K. and MacDonald, L. (2007) *Managing Media Library Intranets*, unpublished (received 16 October).

Nelsson, R. (2006) Credible and Credited: the rise of the media librarians, *Library + Information Update*, **5** (12), 41.

Orlowski, A. (2007) Braindead Obituarists Hoaxed by Wikipedia, *The Register* (3 October),
   www.theregister.co.uk/2007/10/03/wikipedia_obituary_cut_and_paste.
Playfoot, J. (2006) *InfoCentre, IPC Media 2001–2005*, unpublished (15 May).
Schopflin, K. (2003) Net Gain, *Library + Information Update*, **2** (8), 56–7.
Sellors, L. (2007) Personal communication (31 October).
Wales, J. (2007) Post to NewsLib e-mail discussion list (1 November).
Watson, I. (2004) Professionals and Neophytes: librarians, end users and online information (talk given on 24 November),
   www.aukml.org.uk/Ian_Watson.htm.

Chapter 6

Legal issues for news databases and archives

IAN WATSON

One of the key tasks carried out by newspaper libraries since the 1990s has been the archiving of news text to be passed on to news aggregators (or 'hosts' or 'vendors' as they are variously known). Delivering this text has never been much of a priority for newspaper publishers, one consequence of which is that these online archives do not contain the entire content of the printed newspaper, largely for legal and contractual reasons. As the editor and Richard Nelsson have said elsewhere (Schopflin and Nelsson, 2007), the labour-intensive and time-consuming task of newspaper text archiving has been ripe for automating or outsourcing, yet in most cases remains a key in-house activity of the library. Why this might be is explored in the current chapter, which looks at the implications of today's newspaper content being available and searchable via online databases. The author worked at the Glasgow-based Herald newspaper between 1994 and 2006, latterly as Head of Rights and Information. He is currently Knowledge and Information Manager with the Scottish Institute for Excellence in Social Work Education. He is also a noted expert on issues concerning information and the law, in particular online newspaper copyright.

This chapter will describe some of the legal factors that affect the creation and management of digital text archives and the role the librarian may play in these processes. It will look in particular at the 2001 US Supreme Court judgment in favour of freelance journalists whose work was being sold to online news vendors, a key moment in highlighting why newspaper archiving is not straightforward. And in case anyone thought that the issue was settled, at the time of writing (November 2007) members of the US Writers' Guild are on strike because they feel they are not being remunerated for the repurposing of their work on digital and mobile platforms. As media organizations continue to reuse their content in new formats, it becomes more than ever important that somebody is ensuring that the correct metadata is added to it so it is not used for inappropriate purposes. This has to be done by the only people who care about the content of newspaper and television output after it has been published, that is the librarians, archivists and information professionals.

Background

> [T]he newspaper industry still can't see beyond the concept of 'today's artefact' — be it an individual story, which has various rights of ownership, or to the physical newspaper that gets plopped on the driveway.   Tom Johnson (Kenney, 2002)

In this quotation Johnson neatly captures the reason why the online archives of newspapers can be troublesome. In the pre-digital era (say prior to 1985) finding a back issue of a newspaper was not a simple matter for either the professional librarian or the consumer. Newspapers were deposited with public libraries in microfilm and hard copy formats, but search and retrieval involved the time-consuming task of looking up references in printed indexes and then searching for the story. UK newspaper articles were abstracted and indexed in the *British Humanities Index* (*BHI*); www.csa.com/factsheets/bhi-set-c.php), but using the *BHI* was a lengthy process more suited to the pace of scholarly research than the newspaper production deadline.

Media libraries therefore relied heavily on cutting (or clipping) and filing stories from selected newspapers. The entire content of the newspaper was not cut, only key stories selected according to local policy. Useful and popular as they were, cuttings files had some intrinsic defects. Kenney (2002) succinctly describes the state of the average cuttings file:

> A typical news library file would be stuffed with clippings out of chronological order, missing staples and tape connections to continuations that may or may not have been clipped originally. Corrections would not get appended to all copies of a story. Clippings often got put back in the wrong file folder. Files would

slip down behind reporters' desks, or worse, simply disappear and have to be re-created.

As this process did not involve copying or disseminating content, no one had any reason to be concerned about copyright. In the 1980s, however, newspaper production underwent radical technological change, a by-product of which was the creation of text in digital format, opening up the exciting prospect of creating full text, searchable electronic archives. And indeed, most newspapers began to create in-house digital text archives. Some journalists did not like them. One legitimate objection to text archives was that that was precisely what they were: text only. Another complaint was that the original typographical layout was much easier to read than the raw text of the early online databases.

If the user-friendly cutting was no longer available then there were some counterbalancing advantages:

- The full text of the story was now searchable, potentially unearthing a name or place mentioned in passing that would not be picked up either by indexes or cuttings (stories were generally filed under three or four general subjects plus any important personal names).
- Stories could be accessed and read simultaneously (a packet of cuttings could be in the hands of only one journalist at a time).
- Online stories could not be mislaid in the way that cuttings could be.

Initially these new digital archives were seen as in-house resources but the major online vendors of the time – FT Profile (now subsumed into LexisNexis), Mead Data Central (subsequently LexisNexis) and Dialog (now part of Thomson) – spotted the commercial potential and began signing agreements with newspaper publishers to take their data and create online aggregated news archives. The publishers had the data in digital format and the vendors had the technical know-how, marketing, pricing and billing structures in place to deliver the content to the consumer. The vendor would pay the publisher a percentage of the revenue earned (a royalty payment). In the late 1980s the prospects for creating digital archives containing the full text of all newspapers seemed good, and fairly straightforward.

This development signalled a change in the role of media librarians as they assumed responsibility for data feeds to the online hosts, in the process turning the library from a cost centre to a revenue earner as royalties began to flow. Kenney (2002) observed that media librarians became 'voracious consumers of online information sources, as well as providers of content, a perspective that has served them well in negotiating content license agreements for the library's use, as well as in negotiating content sales to vendors'.

Newspaper content

The typical newspaper is an aggregated product, made up of contributions from staff writers and reporters, freelance journalists, stories from news agencies (such the Press Association, Reuters and hundreds of specialized services), syndicated features, letters to the editor and so on. In the early days of online archives few people considered the possibility that the contractual arrangements for the content contributed from non-staff sources might not allow this content to be used for anything other than the printed newspaper. Thus it was not unusual for the entire content of a newspaper to be sent to the online vendors. Michael Jesse, Library Director of the Indianapolis Starr Library, observed that 'Our industry has been pretty sloppy for the past decade or so that we've had electronic archives. Many newspapers sent their entire feeds to Nexis, etc., without even blocking out the wire and syndicated stories' (Kenney, 2002). Indeed it was no easy job to filter out such copy as production workflows often did not record any information about the provenance of individual stories or restrictions on use. The contracts between the publisher and the various sources – news agencies, regular freelancers, theatre reviewers, stringers, astrologists, agony aunts – may not even have been held in one central place, or possibly may not have existed at all.

With the growing realization – in the UK from the early 1990s – that it was not legally prudent to shovel everything onto the publicly available online services, responsibility for filtering out fell to librarians who had to do their best with scant information. Typically librarians would obtain or compile authority lists of what could be put online and what could not. This explicit knowledge was combined with their tacit knowledge of their own newspaper's content. The focus on today's deadline meant that repurposing of content for third parties was seen not as a production matter but as an archiving function to be dealt with post-production, by the library. Some newspapers were aware of the distinction between staff copy and that from third parties, but took the bullish view that the fee paid to a freelancer included the right to include the article in the online archive. This was to prove incorrect and cause a great of trouble in the late 1990s.

Freelance copyright: the Tasini case

An understanding of the interplay between the laws of copyright and contract is a fundamental requirement for anyone working in information management. The Tasini case (US Supreme Court, 2001) was an important landmark in newspaper archiving history as it demonstrates that clear contractual arrangements along with the application of common sense might have avoided some ten years of litigation.

In 1993 freelance writer Jonathan Tasini and others began a legal action against the *New York Times*, *Newsday*, *Time*, LexisNexis and University Microfilms, charging that the publishers did not have the right to put material that had been written for print into electronic media without explicit permission from the freelance writer. The publishers' defence was based on the argument that the files held by the likes of LexisNexis were anthologies of the published newspaper and such use was allowed. In June 2001 the US Supreme Court (2001) finally ruled in favour of the freelancers, rejecting the notion that databases were collective works for copyright purposes. In the Court's opinion, by considering the electronic version of their publications to be simply another edition of the printed work, publishers had infringed the rights of the freelancers. The articles had been disaggregated from the original publication arrangement and this action could not be seen as an allowable extension of the publishers' initial rights. Kenney (2002) provides a concise overview of the case.

In the aftermath of the decision NewsLib (the mailing list of News Division of the American Library Association; http://parklibrary.jomc.unc.edu/newsliblyris.html) buzzed with comment and debate ranging from the practicalities and ethics of purging their public archives to the question of whether this action was in fact in the best interests of the freelancers. Some questioned the rush by the publishers and the online vendors to remove freelance material from the public online archives, arguing they were destroying the historic record. Others highlighted the practical difficulty of separating the 'legal' from the 'illegal' material as the terms under which certain contributors were hired were often lost in history. Some argued that the freelancers had cut off their noses to spite their faces and the newspaper managers were doing the same in respect of the online databases because of fear of litigation. Further, the freelancers stood to lose their personal 'brand recognition', which depended on their work being available online as a kind of showcase: if their portfolios of published work for prestigious publications could not be found online, their public profiles would certainly suffer. Another view was that, although the principle may have been large, the pay-off would not be as the sums of money involved would be small. Elsewhere Tim O'Reilly (2002) has argued that 'obscurity is a far greater threat to authors and creative artists than piracy'. Not all freelance material had to be removed, however, as some newspapers had already reached agreements with freelancers that allowed re-publishing in non-print media. Ultimately the losers would be consumers who just wanted to search newspaper content and had no reason to care about, far less understand, the contractual mechanics that underpin newspaper production.

Tom Johnson (Kenney, 2002) of the Institute for Analytic Journalism at Boston University has argued that a newspaper is just a daily manifestation of a portable database. A good database lets individual users slice and dice the contents and retrieve those contents in whatever way works best for them. Purging that database for short-term legal or financial interests would, he felt, make journalism increasingly irrelevant to the general public. His concern was not about the time and costs of purging, or even the loss of the historical record, it was that the newspaper industry couldn't see beyond the concept of 'today's artefact'. He argued that if newspaper publishers and editors had followed and studied the digital revolution of the previous 20 years, or if they had even started on the problem when Tasini was filed in 1993, they might, by 2002, have had a better understanding of how to leverage tools like metadata and XML, 'the building blocks of a better, more far-sighted journalism and e-news content business'.

In short, the long term preservation of the historic record was separate from the freelancers' argument about payment, which was based on contract law: it was a matter for newspaper publishers to reach contractual agreements that supported their business model. If that business model included online publishing as well as the printed product, then the publishers needed to acquire the appropriate rights through contract. The newspaper business is about repurposing content derived from many sources. That content is someone's property and the terms under which it can be used is defined and determined by contract. Publishers and writers are, however, in a symbiotic relationship. Each needs the other and, like it or not, the terms of the relationship are usually determined in the marketplace by relative bargaining power.

In 2005 a final settlement was reached in which a minimum of $10 million and a maximum of $18 million, less $3.8 million for lawyers' fees and administrative costs, would be made available by the online vendors and publishers to compensate freelance writers whose copyright had been infringed. Although the legal action was brought in the USA, writers in the UK and Australia were also entitled to claim as the 'class' in this class action suit was defined as 'all persons who hold the copyright to an English language written work that, at any time after August 14, 1997, was made available in electronic format . . . without the person's permission by at least one of the defendant databases or participating publishers' (Quint, 2005). As most major English-language newspapers license their content to LexisNexis (one of the defendants), freelance contributors to these newspapers were entitled to claim. The details of the settlement are complex but Quint (2005) provides a useful summary, noting that one set of parties remained without remedy:

> Consumers still turn to databases expecting comprehensive coverage and do not receive it, since articles have been removed or were never entered into the files. The settlement [might] encourage authors to allow publishers and database firms to incorporate missing material into their databases. Since failure to grant future electronic rights permission knocks 35 percent off the fees paid to claimants, the authors should have sufficient motivation. Now, if we could only guarantee that publisher and database firms would rise to the occasion.

The impact of Tasini

According to Quint (2006), although certain categories of information (travel, letters to the editor etc.) have customarily fallen outside the archiving domain of many newspapers, largely as a result of local archiving policies, the result of Tasini is that the online archives are even less comprehensive than before:

> The bottom line is that if a searcher (end user or information professional) goes after everything that a newspaper has published on a topic, the expensive fee-based services could not honestly promise to find it. Even newspapers with the most sweeping archive policies cannot assure the searcher complete coverage. And reference librarians listening to the mournful complaint from clients – 'But I just know I saw it in that newspaper! It must be there. Can't you find it?' – must now simply bow their heads in defeat. No longer can professional searchers claim that a search of the commercial services remotely represents a thorough search of the newspapers carried among their databases.

Ardito (2004) is not certain who has benefited but takes the positive view that publishers and freelancers have learned something. Authors are more aware of their rights and of the importance of negotiating rights with publishers for both print and electronic distribution of articles and textbook chapters. Publishers have been forced to rethink their contracts and have been prevented from continuing 'their decades-long practices, assuming they could republish freelancers' works in any format and in any medium of their choosing without negotiating rights or paying additional royalties to the writers'.

Richard Geiger (2003) of the *San Francisco Chronicle* expressed little sympathy for Tasini. In his view online database revenue amounted to 'pocket change' per story and the newspaper 'will never break even on our payments for online rights'. It was, he argued, outrageous that 'the historical record has been so bowdlerized for so little reason and the damage done to historical archives was out of all proportion to the damage to freelancers'. Geiger of course touches on a key issue underlying the Tasini case: the notion that newspapers publishers were earning vast revenues from freelancers' contributions. Kenney (2002) has illustrated how little value is in fact attached to any newspaper article, freelance or otherwise. She calculates that the publishers might receive a little more than $3 per story per month and that some 80% of stories transmitted in a month might never again see the light of day. When the staff costs of creating and managing the daily feed are factored she calculated the freelancers' share of this revenue at around 60 cents. Set against the initial fee paid for the article (anywhere between $20 and $300) 'it is obvious the value for the freelancer lies in his or her initial negotiation, not in a percentage of online sales through news outlets'. This writer's own experience in the UK newspaper industry suggests these calculations and conclusions are not far off the mark.

The lesson from Tasini is that contract and clarity are important when it comes to handling intellectual property. Bentley (2002) offers a very readable account of the reasons why freelance creators (journalists, photographers, playwrights, musicians, composers etc.) of original works feel they are being treated unfairly and unlawfully by publishers and broadcasters. In the UK the *Guardian* stands out as an example of a newspaper that made positive efforts to reach agreement on the re-purposing of freelance content. In the late 1990s it first published a Charter for Freelance contributors, which has been updated at intervals since then (*Guardian*, 2007). It sets out terms and conditions for the use of freelance copy, which include the non-exclusive right to include the work in internal and external archives.

For the newspaper librarian the process remains complicated. Although some newspapers have created workflows that will generate data feeds to the online vendors that automatically filter out freelance and agency material for which online distributing rights have not been agreed, there are still some in which librarians work from lists cobbled together from human resources and editorial departments. In some newspapers, the production process for online or web editions was able to absorb and automate the creation of data feeds to third party vendors. In others the workflows for these editions tended to operate on the same short term, deadline-driven ethos of the printed page, in which the creation of data feeds was characterized as a post-production 'archiving' task.

Errors, corrections and legal action

Given the amount of information processed daily by the average newspaper it is inevitable that errors creep in from time to time. Hansen, Paul and Neibergall (2003) found that corrections and information quality problems in today's news operations mirror problems and issues documented for more than 60 years by news professionals and researchers. Surveys of newspaper accuracy over the decades have, she found, put the proportion of stories with errors between 40% and 60%, with most hovering at 50%. Errors range from the factual errors ('The Murray-Darling river system empties into Southern Ocean, not the Indian Ocean' – from the *Observer*'s 'For the

Record' column, 12 August 2007) to more serious instances of mistaken identity where, for example, the wrong person is named as being, say, a crooked publican. It is worth noting in passing how much journalists tend to rely on their own archives for factual information, yet can be very sceptical about the accuracy of new media such as Wikipedia.

How a newspaper deals with complaints from the members of the public who feel they have been wronged or who wish to challenge the facts or opinion contained in a story will vary from newspaper to newspaper but in general there is likely to be some dialogue between the editor (or more likely an assistant, associate or managing editor) and the complainant. Some, notably the *Guardian*, publish corrections and clarifications and employ a readers' editor to act as a kind of ombudsman to assess whether complaints stem from a difference of opinion or from a factual error. The *Guardian*'s current readers' editor (Butterworth, 2007) provides a useful summary of the kinds of error that rattle her readers. Correcting mistakes is an important part of her job: under her terms of reference she is required to 'seek to ensure the maintenance of high standards of accuracy, fairness and balance' in the *Guardian*'s reporting and writing and to 'collect, consider, investigate, respond to and, where appropriate, come to a conclusion about readers' comments, concerns and complaints in a prompt and timely manner, from a position of independence within the paper'. Remedies for correcting errors or ambiguities range from publishing a letter to the editor stating the opposing point of view to printing a correction or clarification. If these remedies are not acceptable or appropriate the process may escalate to the point where lawyers for each party become involved in an attempt to reach agreement, possibly including monetary compensation. At the extreme, a case may be brought to court.

What is the role of librarian in this process? Hansen, Paul and Neibergall (2003) found that, in the USA, inconsistently applied corrections policies could cause errors to be repeated and perceptions of news accuracy to erode. In a vast majority of the news organizations, they found, there was no method in place to reveal and correct inaccuracies routinely in reporting after publication. The librarian therefore should ensure that any published corrections are conveyed to the online vendors so that the consumer of the online products has the chance to read the correction; for example 'Weegie Widgets made a loss of £100 million' should have read 'a loss of £1 million'. Online vendors all seem to operate different policies on how to handle published corrections (which may appear some days after the original story) and few seem to be able to append the correction to the original. One solution is for the librarian to append the correction to the original story and resend it to the online vendor. It is important to remember that the contract with an online vendor will contain a clause in which the publisher warrants that the data is not libellous and indemnifies the online vendor against any actions arising from the newspaper content.

Another role for the librarian is to liaise with the editor, managing editor or deputies on upcoming legal matters. When a story becomes the subject of legal action it may be prudent to have it removed from the online vendors as its availability constitutes continued publication, which in effect means the allegation continues to be made. Prompt action to cease making a false allegation can help mitigate any damages that might be awarded against the newspaper.

Although online vendors normally react promptly under the terms of their contracts, aggregators such as Google News, with whom the newspaper has no contract and who aggregate by collecting stories from newspaper websites, create something of a headache as offending material, safely removed from online vendors, may still be publicly available from such web aggregators. Google does provide a facility for take-down requests but it is very nearly impossible to ensure that a story, having appeared on the web, is removed completely from the public domain.

The librarian should resist requests from desk editors or other newspaper executives to physically remove stories from internal databases. Internal databases serve as the record of what was actually published and so are of historic value. When the case comes to court, this copy might prove invaluable as the record of what was actually published. Further, should the allegation be dropped or not upheld in court then the story can be re-instated. It should be sufficient to make sure the story is not retrievable or viewable except by those authorized to see it. Most internal archives will have a facility for rendering selected stories 'invisible' without physically removing them.

Librarians can therefore play an important role as an intermediary between the newspaper's legal department or managing editor and the online vendors. They can take an active role in ensuring that the online offering is as complete and free from inaccuracies as possible.

Live court proceedings

During live court proceedings newspapers should not publish anything that might prejudice the trial, for example information about the accused person's previous convictions or trials. To do so could result in the newspaper publisher and editor being held to be in contempt of court and liable to be fined, or jailed. The process of legalling – where a lawyer advises the editor during the course of the publication cycle of the legal implications of publishing a particular story – generally works well as a process for weighing the legal arguments for and against publishing. The arrival of the web, however, made public access to electronic archives commonplace and raised the question of whether a story in a publicly available digital archive, as opposed to the printed page, could also amount to contempt of court.

William Beggs vs Her Majesty's Advocate

In a Scottish court case in 2001 (High Court of Justiciary, 2001) the judge ruled that material held in an electronic archive and retrievable through a web browser was an act of publication just as much as printing the story in the newspaper. At the opening of the trial of William Beggs for murder, the defence submitted that it was possible to search the web and find material from various newspapers which contained references to the defendant's previous convictions and his character. It was submitted that

> if the material concerned became available to a jury member, the prejudice so created against the panel [the accused] could not be cured by any direction given by the Court to the jury. In all the circumstances, there was a serious risk of irremediable prejudice being done to the panel in the present proceedings. While it was recognized that the Court might experience difficulty in exercising control over the publication of material on the Worldwide Web, to the extent that it could exercise control over that publication, it ought to do so.

The material concerned had originally been published in 1999 and the judge took the view that, had it been published in a newspaper at the time of the trial, then the publication would have been in contempt of court. The question that had to be addressed was whether a website containing archived stories constituted a 'publication' in terms of the Contempt of Court Act 1981. The Advocate Deputy [the prosecution] submitted that in order to find the relevant articles it was necessary to search the website of the individual newspapers rather than simply type the words 'William Beggs' into a search engine. He also submitted that he had obtained the articles on CD-ROM in the Edinburgh Central Library and it would be 'ridiculous' to suggest Edinburgh Central Public Library might be in contempt of court by virtue of the storage of such material. In the judge's opinion the continuing availability of the material was a problem and the fact that it was described as an archive was of no matter as:

> newspapers quite legitimately published the material involved at a time when that act was not objectionable. That published material had been made available in electronic form and remained available at a time when its contents were objectionable. Thus the attempt to argue that the material had become part of an archive and hence was not being published, was without substance.

Archive material made available online, he concluded, amounted to a publication: 'it appears to me indisputable that the material involved here must be regarded as a "publication" or "publications" . . . . Plainly the Websites concerned have been created with a view to the communication of information to the public, or at least a section of it.'

This is potentially very problematic as the implication is that whenever a case comes to court, all references to the accused person's history, including past trials and convictions, would have to be removed from public archives. The judge, however, went on to say that although a story in an online archive on the web was a publication he had to determine whether the material concerned created a substantial risk that the course of justice in the proceedings in question would be seriously impeded or prejudiced:

> It appears to me that the availability of the material as part of an archive, as opposed to part of a current publication, renders it less likely that it may come to the attention of a juror than would be the case if it formed part of a contemporaneous publication.

> Furthermore . . . the material concerned would not be likely to be accessed by the insertion of the name . . . in a search engine. In order to access it, it would be necessary to obtain access to the Website of the newspaper, or other publication which contained the material. Thus, an individual undertaking a random search using the name of the panel [the accused] as the basis for it, would not be likely to access the material.

Finally the Judge emphasized his faith in the ability of the jury to heed his direction:

> At the commencement of the present proceedings I took pains to direct the jury that their ultimate decision would require to be based upon the evidence which they heard in the Court proceedings, and not upon any extraneous matter which might come to their attention. In due course, that direction will be repeated when the time comes for me to charge the jury. I have no reason to suppose that the jury in the present case will not follow that direction. The system of trial by jury depends upon confidence being placed in juries to follow directions which they are given.

Nonetheless newspaper archives still give rise to concerns and in July 2006 the Scottish courts were still routinely advising newspapers of the need to ensure that nothing accessible from or through their websites might give rise to actions for contempt of court. The same logic would presumably apply to archives held on the subscription-based services offered by the likes of LexisNexis.

Loutchansky vs Times Newspapers Ltd

Loutchansky vs Times Newspapers Ltd (Loutchansky, 2002) illustrates a similar problem. In this case, *The Times* newspaper in its printed and online version had alleged that one Grigori Loutchansky (also spelt Louchansky) was involved in criminal activity. The court decided that information published on a website was not subject to the one year limitation rule (a rule that states an action for defamation must be brought within one year of publication). Each time the defamatory statement was transferred from *The Times*' web server to a reader's browser, reasoned the judge, this constituted a separate act of publication. The judge concluded:

> We accept that the maintenance of archives, whether in hard copy or on the Internet, has a social utility, but consider that the maintenance of archives is a comparatively insignificant aspect of freedom of expression. Archive material is stale news and its publication cannot rank in importance with the dissemination of contemporary material. Nor do we believe that the law of defamation need inhibit the responsible maintenance of archives. Where it is known that archive material is or may be defamatory, the attachment of an appropriate notice warning against treating it as the truth will normally remove any sting from the material.

Dow Jones and Co. Inc. vs Gutnick

The case of Dow Jones and Co. Inc. vs Gutnick (High Court of Australia, 2002) raised the question of the jurisdiction in which an action for libel could be raised against a publication on the web. *Barron's* magazine, published by Dow Jones in the USA, alleged that Joseph Gutnick, an Australian citizen, was something of a scoundrel. Gutnick raised an action in Australia but Dow Jones asserted that the Australian courts did not have jurisdiction to hear the case as the publication had taken place in the USA. Echoing Beggs and Loutchansky, the Australian courts took the view that 'publication' took place at the time and place where the offending article became available on the reader's web browser.

These three cases suggest that material in an online archive could give rise to a complaint anywhere in the world regardless of where or when it was first published. It is worth noting that a court may also place some weight on the number of people who might actually have seen the article: see Anonymous (2007).

The Newspaper Licensing Agency (NLA)

The NLA, the collecting agency for UK national and regional newspapers, is a recent entrant to the online aggregator market. March 2006 saw the launch of *eClips* (http://blog.nla-eclips.com), a central digital database of newspaper articles aimed at the press cuttings and media monitoring market. Newspaper content is taken directly from newspaper production systems and processed to present each article, as originally published, in Portable Document Format (PDF) along with a thumbnail image of the page showing the article in its original hard copy context. The NLA is promoting this as a major step forward in the online delivery of newspaper content, benefiting press cuttings agencies and publishers alike. The database currently provides content from the national newspapers as well as key regional and Scottish national content. Another product, *ClipShare* (http://blog.nla-clipshare.com), was launched in 2007 as a desktop research tool for newspaper journalists and librarians. *ClipShare* delivers current and archived articles from the London national, Scottish and regional newspapers in the original context. The articles are made available as text, PDF or set in the page as it originally appeared in print.

These NLA initiatives require the transmission of pages directly from the production system as near as possible to the time when the page goes to print. As this is essentially an extension of the newspaper production process, librarians might not become involved at that stage but they are likely to play a part in ensuring that the NLA is advised of corrections and stories that may have to be removed for legal reasons. The question of freelance content again arises, but the NLA has a scheme which requires the newspaper publishers to pay to freelance contributors a proportion of the revenue they derive from NLA licensing.

Digital editions

Although not strictly speaking newspaper archives, digital editions, that is, digital replicas of the printed newspaper, merit some attention. Two of the major UK suppliers of these editions are Newspapers Direct (www.newspaperdirect.com) and NewsStand (www.newsstand.com). Newspapers Direct also offers a 'print-on-demand' service aimed at individual subscribers, retail outlets, hotels, cruise ships, airlines, corporate offices, libraries, educational institutions etc. NewsStand on the other hand boasts, 'Our paperless distribution service gives readers the closest thing to a traditional print media experience.' According to the UK Association of Online Publishers (www.ukaop.org.uk), whose members include the major UK newspaper groups, digital publications are being developed for many reasons, including higher value for advertisers, lower distribution costs and the possibility of reaching new audiences (Kiss, 2004a and 2004b). The jury remains out on the long term worth of digital editions. Some would question the value of replicating online the columnar layout of printed newspaper when web-based publications can offer so much more interactivity.

Digital editions have attracted some controversy. Although the publisher owns the copyright of the typographical layout, the question arises, as with Tasini, of whether the digital edition is an extension of the printed newspaper or a different format, which is not necessarily covered by the contract to publish in print format. Indeed some freelancers and photograph agencies have questioned whether the fee paid for publication in the printed newspaper includes publication in the digital edition. In the post-Tasini world all parties should be aware of the need for contractual clarity as a way of avoiding semantic debates about media formats.

Conclusions

Why should the media librarian be concerned with copyright and contractual matters? Well, as the opening quotation illustrates, the executives and professional journalists responsible for writing, producing and outputting tomorrow's newspaper tend, quite reasonably, to be preoccupied with immediate deadlines. The media librarian, well versed in the legal framework for information management, is often in a position to take a more considered and pragmatic view of the issues raised in repurposing content. By asking question such as 'Who created this?', 'Where did it come from?' and 'What permissions and conditions of use are attached?', the librarian will impose structure, quality control and long term continuity to the newspaper's digital archive. These are important matters for vendors such as Proquest or LexisNexis whose key selling points include well structured files, going back in some cases to the early 1980s, which can be searched by multiple criteria, including author and date, something that is not readily available on standard web-searching services such as Google. And of course the ability to include multiple titles in a single search is very attractive.

In the emerging knowledge economy, value lies not so much in individual chunks of information, a story for example, but in how information is packaged and delivered to maximize value to the consumer. The world of higher education is familiar with this concept and many universities around the world have made their learning materials freely available on the internet. The rationale for this move is that learning materials in themselves do not necessarily hold much financial value: in the networked economy the real value lies in such things as repeat business, quality of service,

customer relations, image, etc. (Casey, 2006). Newspaper publishers like-
wise need to understand the knowledge economy and place the management
of information assets in the mainstream of their business. Hansen, Paul and
Neibergall (2003) note that in 2003 the US Census Bureau changed the
classification of newspaper publishing from 'Manufacturing' to 'Information
and Communication':

> It appears that the Census Bureau understands, perhaps better
> than news organizations themselves, the changing nature of
> the business . . . . This reclassification of news organizations from
> manufacturing concerns to information and communications
> establishments recognizes that news organizations are information
> processing organisms. They take in information, they digest it and
> they reconstitute it. But as the complexities of this new production
> and distribution environment grow, so do the problems news
> organizations face in the management, usage and optimization
> of their information resources.

Newspaper librarians could be at the heart of this information management
process, which will be increasingly dominated by contractual and licensing
matters. The judgment in the Tasini case (US Supreme Court, 2001)
sharply reminded all parties that business is founded not on copyright but
on contract:

> The Publishers' warning that a ruling for the Authors will have
> 'devastating' consequences, punching gaping holes in the
> electronic record of history, is unavailing. It hardly follows from
> this decision that an injunction against the inclusion of these
> Articles in the Databases (much less all freelance articles in any
> databases) must issue. The Authors and Publishers may enter into
> an agreement allowing continued electronic reproduction of the
> Authors' works; they, and if necessary the courts and Congress,
> may draw on numerous models for distributing copyrighted
> works and remunerating authors for their distribution. In any event,
> speculation about future harms is no basis for this Court to
> shrink authorial rights created by Congress.

Note

The views expressed here are the author's own and are not necessarily those of his past or present employers.

References

Anonymous (2007) Online Libel – to delete or not delete?, *Press Gazette*, (21 July).

Ardito, S. C. (2004) How Are Authors Faring Post-Tasini?, *Information Today*, **21** (4), 22–3.

Bentley, L. (2002) *Between a Rock and Hard Place: the problems facing freelance creators in the UK media market-place*, Institute of Employment Rights.

Butterworth, S. (2007) The Readers' Editor on . . . Knowledge Shared with Good Humour, *Guardian*, (9 April).

Casey, J. (2006) *The Interactive Media Industry, Intellectual Property Rights, the Internet and Copyright: some lessons from the TrustDR Project*, University of Ulster and UHI Millennium Institute.

Geiger, R. (2003) Access to Newspaper Stories: the legacy of the Tasini lawsuit, *Knowledge Quest*, **31** (4).

Guardian (2007) *Guardian News and Freelance Charter* (updated 7 July), www.guardian.co.uk/guardian/article/0,5814,409883,00.html.

Hansen, K., Paul, N. and Neibergall, B. (2003) Survey of Large Newspapers Studies Information Practices, *Newspaper Research Journal*, **24** (4), (Fall).

High Court of Australia (2002) *Dow Jones and Company Inc v. Gutnick* [2002] HCA 56; 210 CLR 575; 194 ALR 433; 77 ALJR 255, (10 December), www.austlii.edu.au/au/cases/cth/HCA/2002/56.html.

High Court of Justiciary (2001) *Opinion (No.2), The Right Honourable Lord Osborne the Cause Her Majesty's Advocate against William Frederick Ian Beggs*, www.scotcourts.gov.uk/opinions/osb1910.html.

Kenney, C. (2002) Newspaper Publishers in the Post-Tasini era, *Searcher*, **10** (3).

Kiss, J. (2004a) Worth the E-paper They Are Printed On, *Online Journalism News*, (10 October), www.journalism.co.uk/news/story813.shtml.

Kiss, J. (2004b) Turn Your Print Into Digital Gold, *Online Journalism News*, (28 January), www.journalism.co.uk/news/story805.shtml.

Loutchansky (2002) *Loutchansky v. Times Newspapers Ltd and Others* [2002] QB 783.

O'Reilly, T. (2002) Piracy is Progressive Taxation, and Other Thoughts on the Evolution of Online Distribution, *Open P2P*, (12 November), www.openp2p.com/pub/a/p2p/2002/12/11/piracy.html.

Quint, B. (2005) Post-Tasini Class Action Case Settling for Up to $18
    Million, *Information Today Newsbreaks* (posted 4 April),
    http://newsbreaks.infotoday.com/nbReader.asp?ArticleId=16234.

Quint, B. (2006) Newspapers on the Run, *Information Today,* **23** (11), 7–8.

Schopflin, K. and Nelsson, R. (2007) Media Libraries, *Survey of British Library
    and Information Work*, Ashgate.

US Supreme Court (2001) *New York Times Co. v. Tasini*, 533 US 483,
    http://supct.law.cornell.edu/supct/html/00-201.ZS.html.

Chapter 7

The regional news librarian: a survivor's guide

COLIN HUNT

Small specialist and regional news libraries face different and often more extreme challenges than their larger, national cousins. At times they are at the sharp end of change, their size making them vulnerable to conglomeration and developments in the industry. Conversely, they sometimes miss out on the technological investment and upgrading which leads to restructure and adjustment in larger organizations. In this chapter, Colin Hunt describes the reinvention of the library at the Liverpool Daily Post and Echo, a local newspaper read by and reflecting a famously characterful and active local population. His story covers more than three decades of struggle, change and innovation.

As he illustrates, regional news libraries are united by their diversity, as their holdings and activities closely reflect their geographical location. However, local news librarians across the world will recognize the opportunities presented by holding niche, specialist collections and the challenge of surviving in an increasingly globalized world. In the UK at least, regional news libraries have closed outright at an astonishing rate in the past ten years. The author's experience shows that with good ideas and strong leadership, they can not only stay open, but the collections and local knowledge held by their librarians can be an important means for their parent organizations to learn about and celebrate the local communities they serve.

Introduction

Newspaper libraries are different. I just didn't realize how different until a summer afternoon in 1973 when I walked into the Dickensian rabbit warren that was the old Liverpool Daily Post and Echo building.

My career until that point had followed the prescribed path for budding librarians in the 1960s: a spell as a junior in the local public library, study for my ALA with day release, sandwich courses and finally a spell as a full-time student at a commercial college. Then followed the move into industrial libraries (as they were then known) with a period at Lucas Aerospace, where Def-Stans (Defence Standards) and the Official Secrets Act ruled. After two years it was on to Imperial Metals, part of the giant ICI group, an information unit at the cutting edge of librarianship in the early 1970s. They were a high-powered, fast-moving department, which each morning delivered the day's relevant press cuttings to the MD's desk by 8.30 a.m. sharp. We worked with research scientists, engineers and management at all levels, and were part of an ICI team implementing early computerized indexes such as KWIC (keyword in context) and KWOC (keyword out of context).

As the interview drew to a close the man across the desk leaned back in his chair. He was an imposing man, bulky but elegant. The broad stripe shirt, club tie, and over-strong cologne perfectly complemented his swept-back steel-grey hair and bristling moustache. His left eye was half closed, trying to avoid the smoke from the freshly lit cigarette that protruded from, judging by the nicotine stains, the regular position under his moustache.

'Colin, I'd like you to work for me', he said with a smile. I mumbled my acceptance. He leaned across the desk and we shook hands. He stood and went across to a grey metal filing cabinet. 'You'll take a drink of course', he said as he produced a bottle of Johnnie Walker and two glasses. That was the moment I realized I would never work in an industrial library again.

Historically the differences between our various regional news libraries are not great in terms of stock and the range of services we provide. The basic skills required in one could be transferred to another, with the exception of one key element, local knowledge. The geography of where we are, the communities we serve and the sense of place that imbues our local media all help define the library's role. This chapter is in no sense a comprehensive academic review of the history and current trends in British regional news libraries. The focus is very much on my own library at the *Liverpool Daily Post and Echo*, a very typical news library, which during my 34 years at the helm has reflected the history and challenges faced in all the regions. Although it is essentially a personal story it mirrors the daily struggles and strategic decisions faced by fellow librarians across the UK, a group of men and women I'm proud to call my colleagues.

The 1970s

The *Liverpool Daily Post and Echo* (LDPE) library was founded in 1918 when Tommy Hudson, a young editorial assistant, was given the task of pulling together the various departmental and individual collections of press cuttings and photographs into one centralized reference library. Gradually the library grew and over time reference books were added, as were photographic glass plates and negatives together with 'blocks', the metal plates used for printing photographs. At that time they were lead-based but they were gradually replaced by ever-lighter alloys until the introduction of photocomposition in the 1980s and the advent of 'pmts' (photo mechanical transfers). During the period of Tommy Hudson's tenure and that of his successor, Fred Lindsay, the nature and work and content of the library changed little.

The arrangement of the material in our regional libraries was one that suited the needs of the parent organization since none of the older established forms of classification such as Dewey or UDC were applicable to news. Unlike the libraries of national news organizations, which generally structured their collections by topic, the regionals went for a structure that emphasized the location of the subject or event, for example: LANCASHIRE: Road Accidents, or MANCHESTER: Road Accidents, rather than ROAD ACCIDENTS: Lancashire, the style used in the nationals. For all of us, nationals and regionals, the essential problems remained the same, trying to organize material that had not yet established its final form. The difficulty was memorably described by Geoffrey Whatmore in a paper presented to an Aslib one-day conference on the organization of news libraries, as 'trying to organize current information while it is still in a fluid state – before its structure and underlying trends become apparent. It is like trying to study geology, before the earth has cooled' (Whatmore, 1973).

The problem of the fluidity of news and the many other problems identified so clearly by Whatmore in that paper, together with many of the others he discussed in his subsequent writings such as the issues of multiple filing and grouped headings, were being overtaken by two particular issues: the changing nature of news reporting and the language itself. Jargon had become an increasing currency of news reporting, with terms such as 'mugging' and 'gazumping' entering the language, leaving many libraries with the problem of integrating new headings and filing new material. Not only was language and the nature of reporting changing but for local newspapers even worse was ahead. Local government in the UK was reorganized in 1974. New authorities with new names were created, old councils with traditional names disappeared or were split up, and new tiers of local government were created. Local authority reporting was, and still remains, one of the staples of the local media and detailed, well organized library records are key to the informed reporting of local affairs.

Regional new libraries struggled while their company managements were generally too remote to understand the issues. The stability of years of diligent work was threatened and as a technology-fuelled society raced ahead, with the media in hot pursuit, regional news libraries languished with their now-outdated procedures and resources, ignored by newspaper executives preoccupied with making their own adjustments to changing circumstances. To paraphrase Philip Larkin's observation on sexual intercourse (I'm sure Larkin wouldn't mind, as a librarian himself he was used to having his work plagiarized), 'the decline of the regional news library began in 1970 between the invention of the floppy disc and the Beatles' last LP'. As the 1970s laboured its depressing course into the nadir of the early 1980s a new mood was emerging in news libraries across the UK. The librarians were about to start fighting back.

The 1980s

The backdrop to a decade of change in the profession was not promising. Newspaper proprietors were feeling the pinch financially as a decline in manufacturing and an economic slowdown hit circulation and therefore profits. Technology in the shape of photo composition and new working practices were seen as the only way out of the slump. A wind of change swept through the industry with the launch in 1986 of Eddy Shah's *Today* newspaper in Warrington, which pioneered the use of colour photography, and a bitter industrial dispute with the print unions at News International (publishers of *The Times* and the *Sun* newspapers) over the introduction of new technology in 1986 and 1987, at the eye of the storm. Many companies began to question the value of the traditional news library and redundancies followed. Although many editors asserted that their journalists could not function without the skills and resources of the library, they were in conflict with the overall strategy of their companies. When it came to the crunch and the editors had to choose between losing a journalist and losing a librarian, there was only going to be one winner.

Regional press groups began to consolidate after takeovers and mergers and local librarians were, for the first time in many instances, brought into contact with their colleagues in other parts of the UK. Peter Chapman, Librarian at the *Northern Echo* in Darlington, organized a meeting of librarians interested in formalizing the loose network of contacts that had sprung up and, as a result, the National Association of News Librarians (NANL) was formed. The relationships between media librarians which already existed in London, through common interests and existing professional bodies, had already been formalized by the founding of the Association of United Kingdom Media Librarians (AUKML). In 1988 the NANL merged with the AUKML, to the benefit of both bodies.

The generation of librarians that had come into the media libraries in the 1970s and 1980s was very different from that which preceded it. Some librarians were qualified; many came from outside the parent organization and brought new ideas and experience with them. This contrasted with many of their predecessors who had fallen into their jobs and tended to regard the library as a fixed entity, not something with the potential to develop and change. While the exchange of information and techniques were key factors in moving the profession forward, it was a turning point for most librarians in the regions when they realized that, whether working in Birmingham, Huddersfield or Cardiff, they were not alone and that many of their own daily challenges were mirrored across the UK. The shared problems did not make the solutions any easier or quicker but they became more bearable. The attitudes of the various regional managements was strikingly similar, and there was a recurring theme: just when the librarian establishes a progressive working relationship with an sympathetic editor or general manager, the company restructures, the editor moves on and the librarian starts from scratch again, trying to create a fresh relationship with a newcomer, a process of 'one step forward, two steps back' every couple of years.

In the news library, technical change brought both challenges and benefits. On the one hand, company managements tended to see the generically termed 'new technology' as a means of increasing efficiency, a term that usually translates into employing fewer staff. On the other hand, librarians for the first time had the potential of working with non-traditional materials, with computer-generated text. Most newspaper groups were slow to grasp the potential of the new electronic material for making journalistic working practices more efficient. A notable exception to this was the *Express and Star* in Wolverhampton, which appointed a senior feature writer, Steve Torrington, to oversee the implementation of a text database produced from the output of the editorial computer system. This was then recycled back to journalists' own terminals and the UK's first full-text retrieval system in a daily newspaper office was born. Sadly it would be another decade before most other regional news groups caught up with Torrington's pioneering work.

All libraries reflect the industries they serve and the media tends to mirror social change more quickly than many. Many regional groups experienced an acceleration in the decline in circulation that had been apparent for over a decade. More worrying was the dilution of advertising revenue. The first local commercial radio stations that had appeared in 1973 and 1974 were well into their stride by the early 1980s, capturing not just listeners but also advertisers. Successive governments compounded the problem by granting further broadcasting licences. The embattled regional press was under attack from another new rival, free distribution newspapers. Initially most were weeklies but in 1984 the first daily free newspaper in the UK, the *Daily News*, was launched in Birmingham. The large groups reacted by launching their own free titles, buying out rivals, or making some of their traditional paid-for titles free. The news libraries, all of which operated in the larger paid-for regional units, were at risk.

The challenges facing regional newspapers focused the minds of their managers and there was an acknowledgement that new sources of revenue needed to be found within the existing business structures. Although obvious business options such as reader holidays opened up new revenue streams, certain newspaper managements realized, after some serious lobbying by their librarians, that maybe there was some sort of market for old newspapers and the current stories and photographs, which were now beginning to be held in electronic form, as well as the traditional hard copy cuttings, prints and microfilm. Newspapers such as the *Northern Echo* started to appear in CD-ROM format and there was the realization that there were unexploited markets such as education.

Other companies saw the benefits of changing the roles for their librarians, now released from manually intensive, repetitive tasks. Although the concept of the librarian as a researcher, as opposed to a person who provides a packet of cuttings, may not be new in the wider world of librarianship, the idea of a librarian being capable of taking on more responsibility for the quality and depth of information provided to enquirers, and even filtering that information, was revolutionary for many regional newspaper managements. For some companies the acceptance of an enhanced information role for the library staff was just too difficult to take. Photocomposition had come to the LDPE in 1981 but, as far as library practice was concerned, nothing changed. We still cut and classified the content of the paper every day. The concept of a digital archive was seen as 'something for the future'.

Reinventing the library

As at many newspapers, company dynamics at the LDPE were changing: editors were more commercially minded, there were more projects launched across departments and, although it was still the centre of editorial activity, the newsdesk's position as lord of the jungle was for the first time under threat. Regional newspapers faced stiff competition from BBC and commercial local radio and regional television news broadcasts throughout the day. Many regionals reviewed their news management policies and decided to provide more in-depth news on key stories at the expense of covering as many smaller stories as possible. As a result, sport and features departments expanded, giving a new lease of life to our archives.

At the same time commercial departments discovered the existence of the editorial library, a potential Aladdin's cave. It was apparent to LDPE library staff that the company was not going to adapt the role of librarians to become researchers, as had happened in comparable organizations. So, in 1984, out of a sense of frustration and as a means of avoiding staff cuts, I proposed a radical redefining of the library's role as provider of commercially exploitable content. The commercial areas we identified as having potential for library involvement were photosales, syndication, exhibitions, book publishing and a business subscription and information services targeted at the local business community, core readership of our morning title, the *Liverpool Daily Post and Echo*.

Our photosales operation at the time was a passive operation, moribund, poorly promoted and inadequately staffed. It was run by a former cleaner who shared the same union as a darkroom technician who chose to take a redundancy package, thus saving one member's job. Like all experienced picture librarians, we knew what our customers wanted and, by devising packages of popular images like historic views or famous footballers, and marketing them successfully as reader offers, we successfully dipped our toes in the commercial ocean. The library had won a small victory. The success of this venture led to the company reviewing its approach to photosales and for the first time invested in the operation, as opposed to looking at it as a by-product of the photographic darkroom. As often seems to be inevitable, the library was subsequently squeezed out of the venture, almost in correlation to its success, but it had at least made its mark.

Just as experience had shown us what members of the public wanted to buy, we could see an emerging demand from other media organizations for information and images. With no background in syndication and the optimism born of ignorance, I spent a couple of days knocking on picture agency doors like an encyclopaedia salesman. Among all the disappointments, I learned a great deal through the kindness of people like Tony Stone and Tom Blau. Eventually we struck a deal with Camera Press, which suited both parties in terms of finance and content.

Like all libraries, most of our stock is never seen by our users, who only see the material that falls within their particular fields of interest. To meet this need, we developed a policy for the use of our holdings at exhibitions. We identified areas of stock that we felt would be of interest and have commercial value, not only photographs but also press cuttings and pamphlets. The main thrust of our activity was in North Wales, linked to the Welsh edition of the *Daily Post*, which is the morning newspaper across the north of the principality. We identified major events such as eisteddfodau, agricultural shows and trade fairs as well as visiting public libraries, schools and colleges even shopping centres. The key element in the Welsh venture was that we co-operated with other departments of the newspaper, not just with editorial, but with circulation and advertising. In most respects it was the most successful library venture of that particular period, as we helped to drive circulation gains, stimulate advertising, create a new market for the sale of historic images, increase current photosales activity and of course raise the profile of the title. From a departmental point of view it was the key enterprise. It was a library initiative, managed and driven by the library, which produced tangible results. For the first time we were regarded as being more than the 'morgue'. We had shown our commercial potential and the ability to work alongside other departments as an equal partner.

Through the library's archive and our involvement with local publishers, history societies and libraries, it had become apparent that there was a new way of looking at the past. Where once the market had been for sepia prints of hansom cabs and sailing ships, now customers wanted photographs of the events within their own recent past, the 'swinging sixties', the end of the national service, the trams they used to use to cross the city. The demand was for what came to be called 'living memories'; we were witnessing the birth of the nostalgia industry. A couple of enterprising authors had spotted this and we produced a number of successful volumes with them using the resources of our library. The cost of these books was borne by a sponsor, Whitbread, so we had the benefits of joint branding and shared publicity. Sadly, not content with half of a very profitable cake, the LDPE decided it wanted a whole gateaux and we started producing books ourselves. Without the necessary skills and expertise, and entrusting the projects to trainee journalists in the mistaken belief that writing such books was easy, they flopped, leading one senior executive to state in 1988 that 'the nostalgia bubble has burst'. We didn't produce any more books until 2003.

Our business subscription service had similar objectives to the exhibitions programmes, that is, to use the skills and resources of the library to generate new business in a number of different areas. The concept was simple, with elements stolen from existing programmes such as the old Financial Times Business Information Service. The target customers were corporate: local businesses of all sizes. The idea was straightforward: customers subscribed to the *Daily Post* at an agreed rate; in return they received a set number of copies of the newspaper, an agreed amount of access to the library for research and a reduced rate on photosales. As an add-on to the package we offered a limited range of commercial photographic services such as business portraiture. Although the initial take-up was good for this scheme it ultimately failed as it became difficult to administer. When we reached the point where a business case had to be made out for an extra photographer to satisfy the demand, it was hard to justify the investment with potential income. The venture was too complex and we had too many eggs in one basket. A valuable lesson had been learned.

The 1990s

Two key events took place as the 1980s turned into the 1990s. In February 1989 Sky Television beamed its first broadcasts via the Astra satellite and two years later the work of Tim Berners-Lee and others at the European Laboratory for Particle Physics (CERN) established a revolutionary protocol for information distribution, which led to the launch of the world wide web. These events were to determine the shape of the media over the coming years.

During the 1980s many parts of the regional press focused too much on the problems that lay ahead rather than the opportunities brought by change. There was also total ignorance of the quiet revolution in supplying text for online databases such as LexisNexis as a potential for new revenues, which national news organizations were exploiting. The 1990s brought its own set of challenges and opportunities. In newspapers throughout the UK the traditional composing rooms, which had long since 'banged out' their final hot metal front pages, were being phased out as production journalists took control over the pre-press operations. Meanwhile, the future was looking increasingly bleak for news librarians as end-users now had direct access to information, which was previously the domain of the librarian. In some companies librarians found a role re-purposing data for online hosts, in others they became information gatekeepers, channels for enquiries. But wherever local media companies struggled financially under the onslaught of multi-channel television, 24-hour news, the expansion of local commercial radio and free newspapers, cuts to library services were an easy option.

By the late 1980s there was general acceptance within the LDPE that the editorial library had a great deal more to offer the company than yellowing press cuttings and dog-eared photographs. However, nothing runs smoothly and a succession of company re-organizations put the library back to where it had been a few years earlier. New editors and commercial managers needed persuasion that the department had value over and above basic services to journalists. In 1997, following the introduction of yet another new editorial system at the LDPE, I was called into the general manager's office to be told that with immediate effect the library staff was to be halved from six to three. Naturally there followed a frank exchange of views and we managed to reach a compromise based on my reasoning that the new system would not necessarily deliver all that the company required in terms of archiving and information provision. A delay in the implementation of the staff reductions was agreed; fortunately the automatic archiving function on the 'new' system was a failure and we survived as a department through natural wastage until the next challenge in 2003.

Not all regional news libraries faced the same challenges in the 1990s. In an account given to the MidAtlantic News Research Conference, Chris Hardesty (1997) spoke about his work as News Research Manager of the *News & Observer*, Raleigh, North Carolina. In terms of circulation and population the area served by the Raleigh group of newspapers is comparable to the region then covered by LDPE's three daily and 26 weekly titles. But by comparison with LDPE's six members of staff, Raleigh had 11 full-time and eight part-time employees, ranging from researchers to data collectors and photo archivists. The Raleigh *News & Observer*, not the best known newspaper in the USA, genuinely appreciated the added-value that a properly staffed library can offer to its publications. This is not a philosophy that has ever been widespread in the British regional press.

The library today

By 2003 the old LDPE was no more, as the company was now part of regional newsgroup Trinity Mirror (TM), which emphasized centralization, synergies and the economies of scale. Common editorial operating systems meant that TM journalists across the north of England had access to the same databases. It was decided that input into the new system would be automatic, with no manual intervention, and all text could be output in formats acceptable to the internet and online databases. The library, now with a staff of three, once again faced an uncertain future. This time the local management took the view that as a news-rich region we should be reaping the benefits locally of any commercial spin-offs from editorial. The City of Liverpool's 800th birthday in 2007 was fast approaching and it would be unthinkable to reduce library staff at such a time. The city had also been voted European Capital of Culture 2008, which would offer its own range of publishing opportunities. In addition to having these key events to focus on, the region was enjoying an explosive period of investment and growth. If ever there was time to maximize the resources of our archives this was it. A team was formed to draw up a commercial development programme to maximize benefit from our archive and current editorial output. For once, the library was at the heart of a project instead of being an afterthought.

This experience has been very much a case of déjà vu, in that we have revisited many of the topics we covered in 1984. The main difference is that the library is no longer within the editorial division in the company structure. As a department, our prime responsibility is, and always will be, supporting journalists across all our titles, but we do this from outside their department. Our journalist colleagues see no difference in the level of service they receive and, in the main, are unaware of any changes, although the majority of staff time is spent on commercial activities. We are very much a hybrid department; I report to the editors on editorial matters and the commercial development director on commercial matters. The new arrangements started in the summer of 2007 and so far the signs are promising. We work closely with our picture desk syndication manager who is also part of the Commercial Development Department and rely heavily on him for all technical matters relating to images, which are beyond our skills. In October 2007 the company appointed a salesman specifically to promote library and syndication products, perhaps the first in the UK regional press. As librarians we see it as a vindication of the ideas we have been promoting for so long.

Our principal areas of commercial activity are now photosales and book production, although the proposed digitizing of our daily titles will also open up new opportunities for us. Photosales is a more difficult market than ever before. Good standard digital cameras and home computers at affordable prices give the non-professional the ability to take quality images with little effort. Whether it is the children's sports day or sunset over the garden shed used by the local television station as a backdrop to the weather forecast, anyone with a modicum of skill can produce satisfactory results. The only photographs that will sell are those the individual cannot take themselves, either because only a press photographer could have access to a specific event or location, or because they are archive images. With this in mind, we have built up collections of potentially saleable images from our archives across a range of subjects, generally following the 'living memories' rule of thumb, the belief that customers would make a purchase if they could relate to the subject matter of the image strongly enough.

The advent of online photosales across our websites gave us the opportunity to be flexible about how we packaged the images. The library has responsibility for developing and maintaining special collections on our websites and selecting the best images from our archives. We can monitor sales, look for purchasing trends then adjust the content of the various categories online. We are currently experimenting with digital photoframes showing great Liverpool and Everton footballers of the past and changing sequences of city views. We also target specific commercial clients such as offices, cafés, bars and new residential developments for prints of archive photographs. We can offer a portfolio ranging from Ikea-style art works to historic views from generic nostalgia shots to a range of surreal montages.

The montages are the products that have finally established the library as an innovative department. For several years the library has had content and design responsibility for our company calendars, due in no small measure to the apathy of other departments to take on responsibility for what was seen as a lame duck and which was even abandoned for a year in 2003. Using our knowledge of current and past material we have produced a series of calendars over the last three years, showing increased revenue year-on-year. The montages were the library's concept for the 2008 calendar, combining some the most atmospheric of our old photographs with just a touch of modernity. Some montages were humorous, some slightly disturbing, some outrageously surreal, but all were thought-provoking. There are any number of individuals with the technical skills to produce this kind of work, but only the librarians have the in-depth knowledge of the stock to produce the original concepts. The idea has also had some success in the corporate market. We have already delivered several large-format montages to a newly opened restaurant, all designed specifically for the customer. We were also able to supply a promotional DVD using a range of new and old photographs relevant to the restaurant and its location.

Having had the contract to produce the match day programmes for Liverpool and Everton football clubs for a few years, the company decided to expand into the sports books market and, using the expertise acquired from this, we started publishing a wider range of material in 2005. We now publish around 30 books a year, ranging from sports books to local biographies and nostalgia publications. In volume terms the most successful publications are the Heritage photographic series, which are library-based publications. Librarians decide the themes, choose the images and, unless specialist knowledge is required, write the captions. The Heritage series started life in 2004 as newsprint partworks in the *Liverpool Daily Post and Echo*, published to coincide with a cover price rise. The collections were so successful, at times putting as much as 10% on circulation, that the concept was transferred to the book publishing programme. As with the calendars, the library inherited responsibility for these publications by default rather than by design. Our two heritage books published early in 2007 have generated revenue of around £120,000 in the first nine months of sale. There will be two new Heritage publications in the first quarter of 2008.

The news library in Liverpool has travelled a long way since the first cuttings and photographs were brought together in 1918, but the fact that we survive at all is testament to the generations of staff who have diligently collected and arranged the material over the last 90 years. Not all news librarians have been as lucky as I have. There was great source material to work with and occasionally editors and commercial managers willing to listen to some pretty wild ideas, and sometimes even back them. To flourish as independent departments in the future, regional news libraries must be proactive. It really is a case of 'back to basics': know your stock, know your customers and, like any good business, bring the two together. The strength of our regional libraries lies in their unique content. Unlocking that content is the key to the future.

References

Hardesty, C. (1997) A Day in the Life, *MidAtlantic News Research Conference, July 18-19, 1997,*
    www.ibiblio.org/slanews/organizations/midatl/97/chardest.html.
Whatmore, G. (1973) Classification for News Libraries, *The Organization of Modern Newspaper Libraries*, London, 23rd March 1973, published in *Aslib Proceedings*, **25** (6), 207.

Chapter 8

Swimming upstream in a media library

CAROL BRADLEY BURSACK

Our final chapter looks at the how media librarians are viewed by their colleagues, the journalists and programme-makers in the newsroom and editorial offices of the world's media companies. The author is a newspaper librarian and elder care columnist living in Fargo, North Dakota, USA. She is the author of Minding Our Elders (2005), speaks on caregiving issues, and has a blog and website, all under the brand 'Minding Our Elders'. In her highly personal account, Carol Bradley Bursack recounts her unusual route from library fan, through life and non-media library jobs, to becoming a newspaper librarian. She gives an honest picture of the way that journalists view the library 'help' and how our status and image can improve when we demonstrate to the news-makers how valuable we are to them. The issues she touches on are increasingly relevant to the modern media librarian. No longer necessarily locked up in our basement morgues, today we attend editorial meetings, train people at their desks and provide expert advice on the spot.

This chapter may bring wry smiles of recognition to the faces of some readers. Never hungry for status, librarians tend to arm themselves against patronizing remarks and downright rudeness by hugging their superior knowledge, skills (and, often, qualifications) to themselves. This book aims to add to that armoury, not just by sharing advice and experience, but with a reminder of how important we are in creating the world's newspapers, magazines, websites and television programmes and making sure people can find them again. If we can celebrate our amazing abilities more loudly, perhaps our colleagues will finally recognize them too.

The librarian: larger than life – gatekeeper of knowledge

I was a quiet child, small for my age, fragile, contemplative, with little to say. My life truly began when I discovered books. I grew up in Fargo, North Dakota, USA. Back in the early 1950s, Fargo was still a fairly small town. I'd hop on the city bus, ride downtown, and get off in front of an ornate brick building called the Fargo Public Library. I'd push through the fortress-like doors and enter the library as an artist enters the Louvre: with a reverent heart. I'd inhale the aroma of aging wood, cleaning wax and musty, seasoned books, feeling a kind of wholeness I felt nowhere else.

Roaming the stacks I'd revel in the ambience of what seemed like millions of books. How to choose? Charlotte Bronte's *Jane Eyre*, Thomas Hardy's *Tess of the d'Urbervilles*, Emily Bronte's *Wuthering Heights*. I'd pile up as many books as I could hold, then approach the tall, wooden checkout desk. The stern librarian would eye me suspiciously as I stretched up on my tiptoes and pushed the pile of books over the edge, toward her. I knew she wondered about my age. But she'd seen me there many times before, and knew I brought her precious books back, parting with them with some pain, but always, always, I brought them back without any new signs of wear.

She'd write my name, then stamp the date. How does one acquire such stature? How does one become a guardian of precious books? How does one become a gatekeeper of knowledge? These thoughts roamed my head. I'd look at her with envy, then struggle back through the library's giant wooden doors, re-entering the world, blinking into the sun. I felt like an alien, out in the world. But then I'd remember that in my arms I held the secrets of the universe. My precious books. The bus would soon deposit me, with my treasures, on the street corner near my house and I'd rush home to hide out in my room and read. I don't recall thinking I could ever acquire the knowledge I'd need to *be* a librarian. I believe, if I gave that any thought at all, I would have felt that was for someone with far greater talents than I would ever have. But I did want to grow up to be a writer.

The military library; Patch Barracks, Vaihingen, Germany

I was 21 years old, in 1966. Patch Barracks, near Stuttgart, Germany, was known as a 'flag base'. Most of the people were officers. There were some enlisted Military Police, but it was an intelligence base, with many high ranking officers. These people tended to be career military and brought their families with them. This was the Vietnam era. The French had ushered out the last of the US military. I was hired, in the library, by a young American woman, whose father was an Air Force General. Sue was in Specials Services, which was not military, but they ran the libraries and service clubs for the military. She had her Masters in Library Science (MLS), and thus was well qualified to run the library. Truly, this job was a gift. A library job, and I got paid for it!

I didn't have my undergraduate degree, but Sue had watched me from the library window as I worked with young children in the Patch Barracks nursery school. That had been the only job open. I enjoyed the children and enjoyed working for Frau Irmgart Klipp, who had run this nursery school for American dependent children since World War 2 ended. However, when Sue, the librarian, asked me if I was interested in working upstairs in the library, I jumped at the chance. I couldn't believe I would get paid to hold mountains of books, smelling as only library books could, finding their proper place on the shelves, helping young soldiers find books to fill empty houses and generals' aides do research. It was a dream come true.

Of course, it wasn't always wonderful. A job is called work because it's work. But, for the most part, I loved it. This library served all ages. We did story hour for the children, so I was hot-headed about the controversy over Maurice Sendak's *Where the Wild Things Are*. I loved that book. For some reason, some adults felt the book encouraged children to disobey their parents. Ah, my first whiff of the 'ban the book' mentality. I savoured the idea of being one of the librarians who had their hackles up over attempts to infringe people's rights to choose what they read. It was a heady feeling. I loved going into the stacks and deciding which author I would concentrate on next. Before me was a heavenly collection of books, and I no longer had a stern librarian telling me that I wasn't old enough to be reading them. I *was* the stern librarian.

We who worked in the library, along with the young soldiers, eagerly awaited the shipment of McNaughton books that would allow us to read current bestsellers from the States. I've never been big on lists, and I've never read books because of their popularity, or lack thereof. But, when those boxes came, we'd tear into them like children into a Christmas box. Their arrival meant work. We'd have to process them, and call the long list of soldiers and tell them the book they'd been waiting for was finally in. But it was always a rush. We were treated like celebrities, we library workers. I dare not say librarians, and I offer up apologies for referring to myself as a librarian in previous paragraphs. Sue was the only true librarian, with her MLS. But, still, I did the work of a librarian. I helped catalogue books. I processed them. I mended them. I shelved them. I checked them in and out. I ordered. I researched for anyone from a private to a general.

In fact I did it so well that Sue left for Spain with her boyfriend, leaving me in charge of working with the base commander on the details of a major remodelling. Even the general treated me with respect. By the time I was ready to quit that job, and go back to the States, I'd gained enough respect to be given an award by the Department of War for my 'outstanding service'. And all I had to do was be myself. To this day, I remember those years and that library with deep fondness. Sue and I still keep in touch. Little was I to know how that experience spoiled me. I was still naive enough to believe that people held librarians in high esteem.

The university library

It's 1976. I'm back in the States and I have my undergraduate degree in English literature. Where would I apply for a job? A library, of course. The only library I could find, with a suitable opening, was at North Dakota State University (NDSU), the very same university from which I had graduated. I didn't have my MLS, and in this library the only 'real' librarians had their MLS. Still, the idea of working there appealed to me. I applied for the only opening, which was in the serials department, and was hired.

Working in serials had its amusing moments. NDSU has its roots in agriculture and has a cereals department. I was constantly getting quizzed when I answered the phone, 'Serials, Carol speaking'. Several times each day, I would explain to someone that they had the wrong kind of serial, and transfer them to agriculture. Quite frankly, I found serials boring. I enjoy working with the public and helping people solve problems. I like the detective work of reference librarians, and I knew, if I ever got my MLS, I would head for reference work.

I can't say we 'non-librarians' were treated well or poorly. I believe it was more that some people were status conscious and others were just good people who liked good people. They didn't care about the status of your job. Still, I looked around for something more interesting (to me). At last, a position opened up in interlibrary loans. I snapped up an application, filled it out and was immediately hired. I moved to my new digs down the hall. Here, I would work directly with students and professors, rather than spend my days hiding out in the backroom, putting serial updates in their proper places and checking them off as they arrived in the mail.

I wonder now, as I look back at those days from a 21st-century view, at how quaint we were. People, students and faculty, would come in to our office, fill out a form for a book or paper that we didn't have in our library, and we would order it for them from other network libraries. The machine we used was basically a teletype machine. I truly enjoyed the people. I enjoyed researching for promising sources. I absolutely loved calling a professor with the news that we'd got an elusive bit of knowledge for his thesis out of what was then known as Red China. It took two years, but we got it! What I hated about the job was the teletype. I'm a horrible typist. I'm fast, but I'm sloppy. With that machine, which punched holes in paper for every character you typed, I was a disaster. With letters and numbers being critical, my error rate drove me insane. I had to do too much work over. But still, I liked the detective aspect of the job. I loved the search. So, I stayed. Until I had children, that is. I then retired to raise my kids and become a freelance writer.

My self-esteem stayed intact, with those humble positions in the university library. I guess, because I could surprise a high-ranking department head with materials he thought he'd never get his hands on. Well, that made me feel good. It also resonated with professors and others that the services we provided were important. So we were looked on as professionals. Of course, there were those in the library hierarchy who were somewhat snobbish toward those of us who didn't have our MLS, but that's just how some people are. I truly felt good about the work I did, and I feel I was treated well.

The media library

After 20 years, two children and seven elders who needed care, I found myself, at age 56, looking for 'real work'. The years between the college library and this point had been taken up with caregiving and a marriage that ended in divorce. I had done a fair amount of freelance writing and had got the coveted by-lines. This didn't help with the job search. Job postings for 56-year-olds who haven't worked in the corporate world for two decades were, shall we say, thin. I interviewed for several jobs and even got a couple of call-backs, but no offers.

Meanwhile, I interviewed for a job at our local newspaper, selling subscriptions in kiosks at local grocery stores. I'll never forget walking through the double doors and into the historic reception area of that old newspaper building. Through years of renovations, they'd kept the gleaming, sculpted wood panelling, which dated back to the beginning of the 20th century. Behind ornately carved wood were the offices of the 'important people'. I didn't expect I'd see the inside of any of those offices, at least not for a good reason. I leaned my head back and stared up at the soaring ceiling. I could smell the history. A bronzed, life-size statue, with the appearance of the 1920s newsboy, greets visitors from a corner. The front page of the paper's Pulitzer Prize-winning tornado coverage hangs on a wall – the tornado I remember so well, as it fell on my 12th birthday, in this very town. I remember a feeling of nausea, then drawing a deep breath and thinking, 'There's no place here for me.' My name was called and I was shown through security and directed to the floor where I'd be interviewed for the sales job. I didn't even feel qualified for that. It was depressing that I was nervous for this interview. I knew I was overqualified, but I didn't feel it. And I desperately needed the job.

The man who interviewed me was a very nice person. He knew I was over-qualified for the job and that I needed full-time work (this was part-time). He even asked me why I was applying (I needed to eat and buy medicine for my son, who has health problems). I needed to start somewhere, and he needed me, so he hired me. I still remember Mark – his name is Mark – saying, 'This is a big place. There's got to be something here for you. Work for me until something else turns up.' Remember this man, because I would not have been a media librarian without him.

I kept working at the kiosks, even though the money I made didn't even pay half a house payment. I forced myself to go to a job fair sponsored by the very same newspaper, knowing most jobs there were in technical fields. I was right. Then, as I was getting ready to leave, I stopped by a booth that I almost missed. I picked up a lone piece of paper, lying next to their advertising. 'Job Opening: Library Assistant', it said. 'So, maybe there is something in that place for me,' I thought.

I filled out the application and turned it in, then went back to the kiosks to sell papers. The phone rang. It was a woman with a husky cigarette voice, asking me to stop by her home so she could interview me for the library job. She was on vacation. She lived a block away from me. She liked my resumé – the caregiving, the book I'd written on caregiving, and, of course, the library background. She also liked that I grew up in this community and that I knew it well. I knew its history. This woman, Andrea, knows the value of a librarian with community knowledge. I walked up to her condominium door, at the appointed hour, on the appointed day. I drove there, because I was afraid a block's walk would mess up my 'interview hair'. I knew her name was Andrea, as I'd seen her by-line on cooking columns in the newspaper, and besides, the application said to report to her.

I offered my hand, we briefly shook, she invited me in, sat me down at the table and offered me coffee. She made a point of saying she had hot coffee for me, even though she preferred hers cold. I took that to mean she was welcoming me. We chatted about our community, things we had in common, and briefly about my library background. She asked, pretty much as an afterthought, 'How are your computer skills?' I told her I'd written my book in WordPerfect (most businesses use Microsoft Word, and I knew it). I also used e-mail, but it was a user-friendly, pedestrian brand. She said that was enough. I knew it wasn't, but she wanted me anyway:

> Andrea said, 'I like your vibes. You're hired.'
> I said, 'I've got to finish up for Mark, before I can start.'
> Andrea said, 'Come in as soon as you can. I always put things off and the person who will train you on the software is only there three more days.'
> I said, 'Okay, I'll learn it in two. I have to finish up for Mark.'
> She said, 'Okay. See you next week.'

I was a media 'assistant librarian'. I would work in a 'special library'.

I found out later that the then editor and his managing editor were furious with Andrea for hiring me. If Mark hadn't backed Andrea up – he told them to 'do yourself a favour and hire Carol' – I wouldn't have got the job. That's my Mark from the kiosk job. I didn't have a newspaper background. I was too old, too, but of course it's not legal to say that, so they didn't. But the library had a history of 'little old ladies' through the years, and most were 'trouble'. The editor and managing editor didn't want another 'little old lady'. They didn't want me. In fact, they had hired someone else. In the end, the other person got a part-time library slot and I got the full-time one. They told Andrea that I had one month to prove myself. They were still angry that she hired me. They still believed the young woman they hired was the right choice. She had newspaper experience.

Andrea was known to be sort of, er, difficult. She didn't like the young woman. Everyone else did, though, including the editor. They were all nice to her. They ignored me. I do believe, to this day, that they thought I'd never last, that Andrea would chew me up and spit me out. I wasn't even worth getting to know. Only one reporter bothered to introduce himself, and everyone who came into the library ignored me. I was invisible. A month later the editor fired the young woman. She wasn't very good about showing up for work, among other things. So, I inherited her work, on top of my own job.

Everything was still new. My computer skills were limited. I had to learn to use very difficult archiving software, along with all the computer basics young people already knew. How I did it, I'll never know. Somehow, I did, though I worked many hours of overtime, much of which I didn't report. I just needed to learn the system and get caught up and on track. The editor said he'd replace the young woman, but he never did. I worked long and hard. Andrea was burned out, and admitted she didn't pull her weight. I did the work of three people. But I had a job and it was in a library.

Still, few people, other than Andrea who loved me, bothered even to say hello. The environment was cold and unwelcoming. I'd see people who were grumpy with me laughing and talking with others, so I knew it wasn't that they were just grumpy people. They didn't want to bother with me, and it hurt. But I wasn't a teenager. I had to earn money and support myself and my son. I just kept coming to work each day, doing my job, and going home ten hours later. I loved learning new things and that helped. Andrea was full of knowledge of the 'old library' with all the clippings and microfilm. She barely functioned with the computerized library, but I studied online and learned all I could. I trained myself in the new, and soaked up everything from the old that I could. Still, I felt like an outcast.

Andrea complained often and loudly about her 30 years in the newspaper library. The library always got the leftovers. The library never had a budget. The library was always the last to know anything. At first I thought it was just her negative attitude. I learned that she was right. The library wasn't viewed as important.

Gradually, the reporters started noticing I was there, at least when I was the only one in the library. They would rather grudgingly ask for help. The attitude toward me, however, was that I was 'the help'. I wasn't a reporter. I wasn't an editor. I wasn't a journalist. I was just 'the help'. I don't think they were aware of the way they came across and they weren't bad people. It's just that they had an attitude. They and the photographers were journalists and made things hum. I was the invisible support, and not very important support, at that.

I did start to prove myself, and the editor and managing editor grudgingly acknowledged that I was the right pick. So, I finally had a little support from the corner office. I thought maybe, by working hard and showing what I was capable of, I would be looked on as an equal by the rest of the newsroom. That delusion was squelched in one quick conversation. We had a features editor who, I knew, liked me as a person. He even kind of respected some of my work. One day we were joking about a new 'super librarian' doll that was on the market. She had her hair in a bun, of course, and wore nerdy glasses. But she was a superhero. The features editor was kidding me about being the superhero. It was a fun give and take chat, until he said, 'Yes, and then super librarian shows she can get the job done with fewer resources and less education than the rest of the newsroom!'

Huh? Less education? Different, to be sure, but less? Perhaps two people in the newsroom had a graduate degree, and he wasn't one of them. The rest of us had four-year degrees. Most of theirs were in journalism. Mine was in English literature. No. I didn't have less education. Just a different education. I've since heard jokes from journalists about the 'easy way out' with an English degree. Strange how they look at me when I get references to Shakespeare and Tolstoy, and they don't. Perhaps I didn't come in speaking their jargon (so why do we have to spell 'head' as 'hed'?). However, I've learned as I've worked. And I'm perfectly happy with my English literature degree, thank you.

But that day, when I heard the remark from the features editor, was the day I realized that it wasn't only me. And it wasn't my education (or lack thereof). Librarians, the people I'd grown up thinking of as the gatekeepers of knowledge, were just 'the help' in a media library. This realization was crushing. I'd lived the librarian fantasy; I'd managed to keep the fantasy alive in two very different libraries. But this one, the third one, the media library, brought down that fantasy. *I* may look at librarians as gatekeepers of knowledge, but the media world, in general, does not. Librarians are, for most purposes, the support. The 'help'.

Meanwhile, Andrea decided she'd had it with the whole business, and she semi-retired. She was working from home, writing history and food columns for the paper. And the managing editor had me writing a 'newsmakers' column that ran daily on page 2, mostly about entertainers. I did notice a few reporters were a bit more friendly toward me. Could it be the writing? It was no-brainer stuff. I wasn't too sure. But I was glad to feel a little more warmth. With Andrea gone, I was the only one in the library. In my two short years, we'd gone from three librarians to one 'news researcher'. We'd had a title change. I didn't mind. Andrea hated it. I even thought maybe the new title would add a little shine to the position. I'm so naive.

I was also, at the time, gently pushing the idea of an elder care column. 'Newsmakers' wore itself out, much to my relief, and I was ready to do some real writing. Elder care is a big issue for those of us in the workforce. With our readership demographics, I thought it was a good idea. I had two decades of eldercare and a book behind me. Why not? Well, it seems that the news industry wants to capture the young audience. Only the old folks care about elder care (and zillions of baby boomers!).

I wasn't making more money and I wasn't getting my column. I'd mastered the library technology, and the newer system was less time-intensive than the old one. I needed a challenge and more money. One day I saw a job opening in the 'newspapers in education' area of our company. It paid more than my library spot. I applied. I was interviewed. Suddenly, the editor wanted to see me. He put me on salary. I'd been hourly and was working about six hours of overtime a week. He told me I was going on salary and getting a nice raise. It worked out to exactly what I was making, with my hourly overtime. I didn't let on that I could do this much math. The clincher was that they would give me my column.

I could tell that this move was made grudgingly. The column was to be short, no more than 15 inches. One question, one answer. The answer was to be provided by an expert, not me. It was going to be buried inside. But, it was a column. Hmm, could the timing have anything to do with the other job I applied for? I knew they didn't want me leaving the library. I knew my stuff. They knew I knew it. And they didn't want to try to find a replacement. After all, I'd replaced three people.

The column was a bribe. I took it. I really wanted to stay in the library, but I needed something to keep me there. This would do it, for now. The column started running and became, quite quickly, a popular item. I noticed a little more respect around the newsroom. Could it be that, now that I was writing – granted I wasn't a reporter, but I was writing – could it be that it gave me more credibility than being 'just' a news researcher? I enjoyed the added warmth, but the apparent reasoning grated on me.

For whatever reason, I gradually gained some newsroom visibility. A major move forward for me came from management. The editor who was here when I started was a good newsman. Not known for being warm and fuzzy, but a knowledgeable newsman. He'd come in to fill the shoes of a long-term editor who had died after two decades in the position. It must be an unlucky spot, because this man developed a fast acting cancer and was dead three months later (he'd been in the position five years). The managing editor left for greener pastures. That left us with a young – as in early 30s young – city desk editor as our leader. It also left our editorial board with a huge overload of testosterone. Our managing editor had been a woman, so she had added a little hormonal balance. Now, she was gone. The human resources person was on the board, and she is a woman. But that was it. I expect that my being a woman had something to do with this, but I was asked by the editorial page editor (who had always treated me with respect, by the way, as he could tell I knew the tech stuff) to be on the editorial board. I said sure. I didn't even know what they did on that board. But it seemed to be a good move. This also increased my newsroom visibility. Again, however, it had nothing to do with being a librarian or news researcher. Every step forward was for a different reason.

Our young leader took the reins and filled in as editor, managing editor or city desk editor. He was told, by the publisher, to pretty much hold the line, while they found a new editor. So this is what he did, on the news side. He was also, for some strange reason, a young person who truly understood the value of a news library, and the value of a news researcher who knew the community, someone old enough to remember things, before they were as they are now. This young man became my supervisor. He also championed my elder care work and encouraged me to go out to give seminars and workshops. He considered me (and still does) a good ambassador for the paper. I've since, successfully, blended the two jobs, and feel very lucky to have a manager who respects both of them.

Back to leadership. The search was on for a new executive editor. A woman was hired. She disliked me instantly. She absolutely couldn't figure out why a news researcher was at the news huddles and, worse yet, on the editorial board. But by then I'd garnered enough credibility with the publisher, and others, that she stopped her snotty treatment of me (rather suddenly, I thought – was she told to change her ways?). She lasted a little over a year and was fired. The young man who took over the job of editor/managing editor finally got what he deserved – he became our executive editor. And a bit of a local hero, I might add, as he'd started at that newspaper as a paper carrier, when he was a kid, and now he was at the top.

Gaining respect

Through all of the drama in the newsroom, death, replacements, firings, I felt my credibility rise. Maybe it was just that I was a constant in all the turmoil. Was there perhaps just a little more respect for what the library had to offer? Maybe I was just imagining it. I've noticed since that time, however, whenever we get a new reporter, he or she usually starts out treating me like 'the help'. After a bit of time, usually after I've pulled a rabbit out of a hat and got them through a journalist's nightmare, they've changed their attitudes. But it's a one-by-one conquest.

Just these last few months, our community has observed three fairly major anniversaries: a 100-year flood (10 years), the sailing of a primitive ship from Minnesota to our sister city in Norway (25 years) and a devastating tornado that killed a dozen people (50 years). These events, all of which I lived through and have personal historical knowledge of, have given me a spotlight, of sorts, to help the library shine. In particular, commemorating the tornado brought me to the forefront. Not only was I the only newsroom employee (other than Andrea, who was still working from home writing columns) who had lived through the tornado, I was old enough to remember it. We did some heavy duty coverage, all of which depended on library materials, library research and even my personal memories. The project was a huge success. I do think that it surprised a few young reporters, to learn my age (since the event was on my 12th birthday, and I wrote a column about it, it's not hard to do the math: I was turning 62). But more so, I believe it educated them about the true function of the newsroom library.

Young reporters are used to everything being electronic and, in general, feel they can search as well, if not better, than I can. After all, they are journalists, educated in the era of computers. Most have the mindset that everything is on the internet. What do they need me and my dusty old files for? So, few turn to me for help in electronic searches, unless they are truly stumped or we are having problems with our internal system. This June, however, many young reporters experienced, for the first time, the spine-tingling awe of staring down at the actual copy that won our newspaper a Pulitzer Prize. A fragile, yellowed record of a tragic moment in time, remembered only by those of us with many decades under our collective belt. The 'librarian' had dug up this original newspaper from the bowels of this old building. Some other long-forgotten librarian, a half-century ago, had the foresight to save some of these precious issues.

On the front page of this old paper, the reporters saw, in black and white, the amazing photo of one young man, from the poorest section of town, standing in the rubble, holding the battered body of a dead child. I do believe the opinion of many young news people shifted just a bit, during this time. 'Ah, the library isn't just where I go to pick up a copy of today's paper. It's not just where I go to complain when the archive system isn't searching right, or to find a road atlas. The library, and even, perhaps, the librarian, helped us pull off some of the most memorable reporting we've done for several years.'

What does all of this really mean? Unfortunately, it means to me that little has changed. The respect I've garnered over these years has come more for my writing than my librarianship. I'm not complaining about the writing. I am a writer and I am happy to be recognized for my contributions. But the media librarian, now more commonly called the news researcher, still has much to prove, before he or she is considered anything but a backdrop on the stage of journalism. Each media librarian seems to have to start from scratch, and trudge a long, complicated road toward getting his or her due respect. The media librarian is still swimming upstream.

References

Bursack, C. B. (2005) *Minding Our Elders: caregivers share their personal stories*, McCleery and Sons.

Index